AF880871

NEWTON PAGE

NEWTON PAGE

JOSIAH CHILD

THE COMPLETE WORKS:

ECONOMICS AND TRADE

VOLUME I

By

Sir Josiah Child

Edited by

Gavin John Adams

NEWTON PAGE

NEWTON PAGE

www.newtonpage.com

Josiah Child
The Complete Works:
Economics and Trade
Volume I

By
Sir Josiah Child
Edited by
Gavin John Adams

A Discourse About Trade, Wherein the Reduction of Interest of Money to 4 l. per Centum, is Recommended. (1690)

Published by Newton Page 2019

1 3 5 7 9 10 8 6 4 2

ISBN 978-1-934619-20-9
Library of Congress Control Number: 2019948530

Published in the United States of America, Louisville, KY.
Set in Adobe Garamond Pro

CONTENTS

NOTE ON THE TEXT

Since each of the books and pamphlets contained in both volumes of this collection were first published in the late seventeenth-century, conventions of spelling, grammar, punctuation, expression, vocabulary and general notation have each undergone considerable modernization. In addition, the relatively crude practices of seventeenth-century book and pamphlet production have been gradually replaced by the radically more exacting standards of modern publishing, which demand both uniformity of typesetting and editorial consistency. As a consequence of those changes, the modern reader is used to a more polished product than those available in the past.

However, notwithstanding the usual expectations of the modern reader, and in full appreciation that the original texts are not as easy on the modern eye as they would have been on their contemporary equivalents, the temptation to edit them to conform with modern writing and publishing conventions has been resisted. That approach has been taken because to do anything other than retain the original form of the texts would be to detract from their colorful character. The only two minor exceptions to that approach have been the correction of dischordant italics and the replacement of the medial s with the modern s.

Each of the books and pamphlets were written for the consideration of the inhabitants of Great Britain. As such, each is tailored to conform with the conventional seventeenth-century stylistic expectations of a British readership. American readers will notice that in maintaining the integrity of the original publications, the original historic British forms of spelling have been retained. More generally, readers will notice both inconsistent and imaginative forms of spelling throughout.

Reproduced in this Volume I of the collection is the first edition and printing of:

A Discourse About Trade, Wherein the Reduction of Interest of Money to 4 l. per Centum is Recommended (1690).

A DISCOURSE ABOUT TRADE,

Wherein the Reduction of Interest of Money to 4 *l. per Centum*, is Recommended.

Methods for the Employment and Maintenance of the Poor are proposed.

Several weighty Points relating to Companies of MERCHANTS.

The Act of NAVIGATION.

NATURALIZATION of Strangers.

Our WOOLLEN MANUFACTURES

The BALLANCE of TRADE.

And the Nature of Plantations and their Consequences in relation to the Kingdom, are seriously Discussed.

And some Arguments for erecting a Court of Merchants for determining Controversies, relating to Maritime Affairs, and for a Law for Transferrance of Bills of Debts, are humbly Offered.

Never before Printed.

Printed by *A Sowle*, at the *Crooked-Billet* in *Holloway-Lane*: And Sold at the *Three Keys* in *Nags-head-Court*, *Grace-Church-Street*, 1690.

A

DISCOURSE

ABOUT

TRADE,

Wherein the Reduction of Interest

of Money to 4 l. per Centum, is

Recommended.

(1690)

A DISCOURSE ABOUT TRADE

THE PUBLISHER
TO
THE READER.

A DISCOURSE ABOUT TRADE

THE PUBLISHER TO THE READER.

The following Sheets were wrote, as the Reader will observe by the Contents, soon after the dreadful Fire, which happened in London in the Year 1666. they fell very accidentally into my Hands in Manuscript (as they had ever since continued) this last Summer, and having, in my Conversation in the world, heard several of the Propositions therein discussed, frequently contrasted, I did set my self with some Curiosity to run them over, and in doing it, discerned (as I thought) much experimental Truth and Reason, and a more then ordinary Life and Spirit, for the Publick good, in the whole Work; I therefore made suite to the Judicious & Worthy Author, to permit me (to the same end for which it appears to have been at the first wrote) to hand it over to some of our best Patriots, to which he being pleased to concede, I began to transcribe it, but finding that that would prove a tedious task, and that that way would confine this excellent Treatise to too narrow bounds, I have presumed thus to emit it to the World.

I may not divulge the Author's Name, but this I may

truely say; He is no Trader, neither pays any Use for Money, but receives a great deal yearly, and hath to my knowledge a considerable Estate in Lands, and therefore the most invidious cannot conceive he had any private or selfish end in the following Discourses.

I have in my time been privy to, and frequently concerned in the buying and selling of much Land, and I find every thing he said at that time so true of the then low Rates of Land, as was his Prediction of its rising in Purchase so soon as that lazy way of Usury by Bankeering should be broke, that I am morally confident if the Parliament should be pleased to abate the Interest of Mony by a Law to 4 l. per Cent. We shall as certainly see Lands in England as generally sell at twenty five years Purchase within five years after such a Law, as We did see them about the time the following Discourse was Wrote, sell at seventeen years Purchase; and as We do now see Lands currently sell at twenty years Purchase and upwards.

I took occasion in my discourse with the Author, to observe to him, that though Lands in general were risen in sale, as he fore-saw, to twenty years purchase or more, that yet Marsh and Feeding Grounds were abated in Rent to the Tenants, at least 20 or 30 l. per Cent. He granted me to be in the right herein, and imputed the cause thereof partly to the Prohibition of Irish Cattle, and partly to the late general practice of sowing Clover, Saint-foyne, Rye-Grass, and other Grass-Seeds; upon which I ask'd him, Whether he thought it would not tend to the publick Good, to prohibit by a Law the sowing of those Seeds? He said by no means; Honest Industry and Invention is never to be obstructed by Laws. I queried then, why Usury should be checkt by a Law? He replyed, that in the Trade of Usury there was neither Industry not Invention, but Idleness and Oppression; and that all Christian Churches, as well as most particular eminent Divines ever since our Saviour Christ's time, had condemned Usury as sinful.

The fore-going Discourse leads to another great Question; Whether Foreign Commodities, such as tend to nourish Vice and Luxury, ought not for the publick Good to be prohibited by a Law, or by loading them with a deep Custom; such as Wines, Brandy, Sugar, Tobacco, &c. And I am humbly of opinion, with the most profound submission to all my Superiours, whose proper Business it is to agree and constitute Laws, that it is not for the publick Good to load, even such Commodities, with so great a Duty, as doth, or may ruin our Plantations, or totally prevent the English from a possibility of supplying the Eastern and other parts of the World with these Commodities, because by so doing, We give away (the most precious of all our Trades) a great part of our Navigation, to our wiser Neighbours the Dutch, who had rather pay their Twentieth Penny twice a year, than loose their Trade to the Baltick with Salt, Wine, Brandy, Tobacco, &c. I might say, too, with Chesnuts and Walnuts, as inconsiderable as their value is; Every thing being to be prized above Gold, that encreaseth the Navigation of any Country, especially that of this Island of England.

I have been always an Advocate for Liberty, and an Enemy to Persecution for matters of Religion, and so I am confident was the Gentleman, our worthy Author, as the following Tract clearly evinces, and by so doing gives the Reason why this admirable Work hath till now lain in obscurity, the Policy and Councils of the late Reigns constantly discountenancing that excellent Principle: And because Liberty of Conscience is frequently touch'd in this ensuing Discourse, and declared to be a principal means to advance the publick Good of this Kingdom, (viz.) Trade; Which 'tis evident is the real and only design of this Treatise, I shall take the freedom to tell my thoughts very plainly in relation to it.

I remember that greatest Master of Historians, Cornelius

Tacitus says of the incomparable Roman Emperour Nerva, that he did Reconcile (Res olim insociabiles) things never before adjusted, the freedom of all Men, with the sole Command of one. Such a Prince, I hope and verily believe God Almighty in abundant Mercy to this poor Nation, hath sent us in his present Majesty, our truly good and gracious Soveraign King William, (the Favourite of Heaven, and Delight of Men) under whom We may most undoubtedly be the Happiest People upon the Face of the whole Earth, if We will; but We shall never attain that Happiness, and hand it over to Posterity, except We all, as well Dissenters, as Church of England Men, do sincerely and cordially endeavour to imitate the Wisdom and Goodness of that Memorable Prince Nerva, to reconcile things formerly unsociable (viz.) Liberty of Conscience to all, with the preservation of one entire Uniform National Church, in the enjoyment of all the publick Revenues thereof; these two things, in my most unbiass'd, retired thoughts, are so far from contradictions, that (as our People in England are now, and have been for two or three Ages past divided in Opinions) they are necessary Relatives one to the other, and neither of them can stand long alone without the other; Time, in innumerable instances having proved it a most manifest Error, in our Kings, Lords and Gentlemen, that they attempted by Laws to compel all the People of England to a Conformity to the National Church; And no less Error was it in the Dissenters and their Adherents in the late Civil Wars, to think to enjoy long the Fruits of their Fighting and Conquests, by keeping all Forms of Religion loose and equally capable of preferment to the publick Revenues, without Establishing any National Church, the publick Revenue whereof, none should be capable of enjoying, but such as were of it.

Many of the Dissenters are so ingenuous as to confess this to be a very great Truth, and that England cannot long enjoy a lasting Peace and Quietness without it: But then they say, Open your Church-Doors wide, remove all stumbling Blocks, & such things as give offence to pious and learned Men, in your Articles, Canons and Liturgy; and probably I may herein incline to be of their Opinion. But yet I tell them, I am a Subject, and have now by Law a liberty to worship God, as I think he ought to be worshipped, and enjoying that, 'tis my Duty in Reason as a Man, and in Religion as a Christian to acquiesce without murmuring; that the King, Lords and Commons (who are the natural and proper Legislators of England) should enjoy the Liberty of their Consciences, to contrive or settle such a National Church as they shall think fit, and in their Judgments most agreeable to the Scriptures, and the publick Peace of the Kingdom; and methinks he that is not satisfied with this, doth apparently violate that righteous Rule of our Saviour of doing as he would be done unto.

2dly, Such dissatisfaction at what our lawful Superiors do in this matter of Religion, while we enjoy our own Liberty, may be deemed, and will by many be said to proceed rather from Faction, Covetousness or Ambition, than from pure Religion.

But some Dissenters are ready to reply, Why should we be kept out of the publick Employments of our Country? Are not we as good Protestants, as great lovers of our Country, as virtuous in our Lives, as diligent and inoffensive in our Callings, and as true to the present Government, as any Church of England Men whatsoever?

I say, admit all that, (and I cannot upon this occasion forbear to say, what I have often declared, That I do believe that the Protestant Dissenters are to a Man throughout England true to that Government which the divine Providence hath most mercifully & miraculously set over us) yet you being private Subjects, and having the liberty of your own Consciences, you are not to disturb the present Government settled by your lawful Legislators, but must allow them (your Governours) the liberty of their Consciences in settling the National Church, or you are unjust in the sight of God and Men: When you are called to the Parliament, then you will have the freedom of declaring your Opinions as you think fit.

2dly, I tell them, great Mutations upon a sudden in the Fundamentals of Government, such as changes in the National Church, are dangerous to the publick Peace, and that our Superiors being placed upon the advantage of a better prospect, can see the danger in a better light, and at a more remote distance then we, who converse only in the Valleys.

3dly, That many Gentlemen who bear no unkindness to the Dissenters, are yet affraid of their fickle uncertain tempers, not having forgot that after our late Civil Wars when the Power was mainly in their own Hands, they themselves made several Governments, yet were never long contented with any of their own Creation.

4thly, That they are not yet agreed among themselves what the Errors or Stumbling-blocks in the Church of England are, that they would have amended or removed.

5thly, I tell them that this repining temper at the determinations of Superiors, in them who are at perfect ease themselves, as to their Liberties and Properties, looks very like the Spirit of Persecution, against which they have always appeared to contend.

Lastly, To conclude this subject, for the love I bear to all my honest Country-men, as well of the one perswasion as the other, I pray the Church of England Men to be indulgent to the Dissenters, and I entreat my old Friends the Dissenters, to put on Patience, and not to censure or repine at the Acts of their Superiors, but to hope and expect, that God who hath wrought this late most signal deliverance for them and the Nation in general, and who hath secured to them by Law the

Liberty of their Consciences, which they could never obtain, by all their Fightings, Strivings, Victories and Conquests, will in his due time give them such favour in the Eyes of the King and Parliament, that they may be admitted by degrees into such publick Trusts and Employments, wherein they may not be judged dangerous to the National Church or State.

A DISCOURSE ABOUT TRADE

THE PREFACE

A DISCOURSE ABOUT TRADE

THE PREFACE

The following Answer to that Treatise, entituled, Interest of Money mistaken, I wrote long before the last Session of Parliament, that began the 19th of October, 1669. but foreseeing that that Session might be engaged in greater Debates of another Nature, and in consequence not have leisure to consider this subject, I deferred the Printing of it, since which I have seen another Treatise, wrote by Thomas Manly, Gentleman, endeavouring to prove, That it will be for the advantage of this Kingdom, to continue the Interst of Money at 6 per Cent, but after several perusals of his Treatise, I must needs say, that either I understand nothing of this subject, or else this Gentleman is the greatest Stranger to it that ever undertook to discourse it, he having writ much, but in my Opinion nothing to the purpose, more than was much better (though brieflier) said by the Author of the fore-mentioned Treatise, out of which most of his seems to be borrowed, though the Words be varied, with some additions of Interrogations, Expostulations, Similes and Circumlocutions.

Besides, the Gentleman taking up things at random, and for want of a due understanding of the matter, is very unfortunate in his Instances of Fact, viz.

In his Preface, about the middle, his Words are, Has Abatement of Usury, or some other sublime Policy, obliged the French of late to set upon Trade and Manufactures? And then he affirms, that I dare not touch on that String, in regard that Nation hath not for many Years altered Interest from 7 per Cent.

To his Interrogation, I answer possitively, that the Abatement of Usury hath done it; and if you will not believe me, read the French Edicts themselves, and they will tell you so (an Abstract of one whereof I have recited in the following Treatise.

To his Affirmation, that I dare not touch upon this String, I say, I dare do it, and put the whole issue upon this, for the French in fact have brought down the Use of Money under 6 per Cent, and that to 5 per Cent lately; as I have been credibly informed, and do believe; and if they had omitted this, all their bussling in other things would signifie very little in conclusion.

The Sweeds likewise since they established their Council of Trade, and set themselves to the consideration of making themselves considerable by Trade, have reduced their Interest from 10 to 6 per Cent.

His following Words are, Do Italy and Holland owe their Trade and Riches to the lowness of Usury, or to th ir innate Frugality, wonderful Industry, and admirable Arts, &c?

I answer; low Interest is the natural Mother of Frugality, Industry and Arts, which I hope the Gentleman's Eyes will be open enough to see by that time he hath read a little further, and considered two or three Years longer.

But it may be said, How can a low Interest be the natural Mother of Frugality, when, if this Gentleman be to be believed, Abatement of our Use-Money brought in our Drinking? which he does not only say, but prove, as he thinks, by an instance of Fact; for he says, we now spend usually twenty thousand Tuns of French Wine, (and he believes that a far greater quantity is yearly Imported) and that the computation of Spanish, Rhenish and Levant Wines far exceeds the former, so that by his calculate, & as he says, grounded upon a very good authority, viz. a Report to the House of Commons, it should seem that there is about the quantity of forty five thousand Tuns of Wine of all sorts Imported annually into England.

But if it shall appear in Fact, that before the last abatement of Interest from 8 to 6 per Cent, we did usually import near twice the quantity of Wines annually we now do, and that now in all sorts of Wines we do not import above the quantity of twenty thousand Tuns yearly; then what will become of his large Structure, built upon a Sandy Foundation?

Reader! this is the Case, and the matter of Fact truly recited by me, (which many of the honourable Members of the House of Commons well know) and mistaken by him; from whence I might with much more reason infer, that the abatement of Interest drove out our Drinking (so pro tanto it did) but I know there were likewise other Causes for it, especially the additional Duties that from time to time have been laid upon Wines.

But before I part with the Gentleman on this point, I must note to him another monstrous mistake in Fact, or at least in his Inference, viz. he says, that twenty thousand Tuns of French Wines at 2 s. 8 d. per Gallon, amounts to 640000 l. and concludes (if I understand him) that so much is lost to England; whereas, were the matter of Fact as he supposeth, which it is not so in any measure, this inference would be strangely erroneous; for by the expence of such quantity we can rationally lose only the first cost, which is but about 6 or 7 l. per Tun, and that amounts to but 120000 l. or 140000 l. at the utmost, all the rest being Freight, Custom and Charges paid to the King, and our own Country-men, and consequently not lost to England.

To conclude this Head, I do agree fully with the Gentleman,

that Luxury and Prodigality are as well prejudicial to Kingdoms as to private Families; and, that the expence of foreign Commodities, especially foreign Manufactures, is the worst expence a Nation can be inclinable to, and ought to be prevented as much as possible, but that nothing hath or will incline this or any other Nation more to Thriftiness and good Husbandry, then abatement of Interest, I think I have proved in the following Discourse, and that therefore all that this Gentleman hath said about Luxury, &c. is against himself, and for lessening of Interest.

The Gentleman at the beginning of his Preface saith, He will not enquire into the lawfulness of Interest, but leave the scrupulous to the several Discourses made publick on that subject. For my part I shall agree with him in that likewise; And to the intent that what hath been made publick formerly may the better be known, I would entreat those that would be throughly satisfied therein, diligently to peruse an excellent Treatise, entituled, The English Usurer, or Usury condemned, being a Collection of the Opinions of many of the learned Fathers of the Church of England, and other Divines, Printed at London, Anno 1634 & now about to be Reprinted.

But upon this occasion I shall humbly presume to say, that if by the following Discourses it shall appear, that the Interest of England being higher then that of our Neighbour Country, it doth render our Lands (our common Mother) of vile and base esteem; doth prevent the cultivation and improvement of our Country, as otherwise it might and would be improved; doth hinder the growth of Trade and imployment and encrease of the Hands of our Country; doth encourage Idleness and Luxury, and discourage Navigation, Industry, Arts and Invention; then I make no question but the taking of such an Interest as exceeds the measure of our Neighbours, is Malum in se, by the light of Nature, and consequently a Sin, although God had never expresly forbid it.

But the Usurer may say, suppose the Borrower makes 12 per cent of my Money, is it a Sin in me to take 6 per cent of him? I answer, between them two there may be no commutative Injustice, according to my weak Judgment, while each retains a mutual Benefit, the Usurer for his Money, the Borrower for his Industry; but in the mean time if the Rate given and taken exceed the Rate of our neighbour Nations, these fatal National evil Consequences will ensue to our common Country by such a practice, which therefore I conclude to be Malum in se: And peradventure therefore the Wisdom of God Almighty did prohibit the Iews from lending upon Use one to another, but allowed them to lend to Strangers for the Enriching of their own Nation, and Improvement of their own Teritory, and for the Impoverishing of others, those to whom they were permitted to lend, being such only whom they were commanded to Destroy, or at least to keep Poor and Miserable, as the Gibeonites, &c. hewers of Wood, and drawers of Water.

I purpose to do the Gentleman that right as not to omit taking notice of any thing he hath of novelty in relation to the present Controversie, whether it be material or no; and in order thereunto, the next thing I observe new in his Treatise, is, Page 9. It is, saith he, Dearness of Wages that spoils the English Trade, and abases our Lands, not Usury; and therefore he propounds the making a Law to retrench the Hire of Poor mens Labour, (an honest charitable Project, and well becoming a Usurer) the Answer to this is easie.

1st, I affirm, and can prove he is mistaken in fact, for the Dutch with whom we principally contend in Trade, give generally more Wages to all their Manufacturers by at least two Pence in the Shilling, then the English.

2dly, Where-ever Wages are high universally throughout the whole World, it is an infallible evidence of the Riches of that Country; and where-ever Wages for Labour runs low, it is a proof of the Poverty of that place.

3dly. It is multitudes of People, and good Laws, such as cause an encrease of People, which principally Enrich any Country; and if we retrench by Law the Labour of our People, we drive them from us to other Countries that give better Rates, and so the Dutch have drained us of our Sea-men and woollen Manufacturers; and We, the French of their Artificers and Silk Manufacturers, and of many more we should, if our Laws otherwise gave them fitting encouragement, whereof more in due place.

4thly, If any particular Trades exact more here then in Holland, they are only such as do it by vertue of Incorporations, Priviledges and Charters, whereof the cure is easie by an Act of Naturalization, and without Compulsitory Laws.

It is true our great Great-Grand-Fathers did exercise such a Policy of endeavouring to retrench the price of Labour by a Law (although they could never effect it) but that was before Trade was introduced into this Kingdom; we are since, with the rest of the Trading World, grown Wiser in this matter, and I hope shall so continue.

The next new Objection the Gentleman hath, is Page 13. If we abate Interest (said he) will not the Hollander take the same course, while we like Children wink, and think no body sees us?

Yes, certainly the Dutch will take the same course, except they leave their old wont, for we never yet abated our Interest, but they soon abated theirs; but what if they do? We having brought our Interest to 4 per cent, shall have them against a Wall, we know the length of their Tedder, they cannot run much farther from us, so that if we wink, it is not like Children as the Gentleman supposeth, but if we take his Advice, we shall wink like Children, while other Nations strike us by abating their Interest.

2. If we cannot gain all we would of them presently, we shall gain the more from other Parts of the World, that cannot suddenly abate their Interest to any proportion with ours.

3. Why shall we absolutely conclude that other Nations will do it? May we not think that some Parts or People in the World, may be as un-fore-seeing as this Gentleman pretends to be, and not know it is for their Advantage to lower their Interest, though we know it to be ours?

4. Why may we not think that Corruption, Avarice and Usurers, may be so prevalent in some parts of the World, as to obstruct so good and National a Work as this?

I omit several other Errors in fact that the Gentleman is guilty of in the course of his Writing, and must needs be so, having taken up his notions (for want of Experience) upon trust from others, who perhaps understand as little as himself, viz. Page 16. he saith, Our vent into Spain and Portugal is greatly lessened, and consequently he reckons them two Trades, among others lost in whole or in part, so great a mistake, that I dare affirm, and appeal to the Record of the Custom-House Books, for a judgment in this case, that those two Trades, as to our native Exportations are more then treebled within less then 30. years.

Page 21. he saith, that, If Wages, &c. were as cheap, and Usury as low with us as in Holland, yet if our Merchants live at so great a rate as now they do, how is it possible we should thrive on as easie Gains as those who spend so much less, and Trade so much more?

I answer, there is nothing in the World will engage our Merchants to spend less and Trade more, than the Abatement of Interest, for the subduing of Interest will bring in multitudes of Traders, as it hath in Holland, to such a degree that almost all their People of both Sexes are Traders, and the many

Traders will necessitate Merchants to Trade for less Profit, and consequently be more frugal in their Expences, which is the true reason why many considerable Merchants are against the lessening of Interest, whereof I have said somewhat more in the following Treatise.

Page 43. he propounds another remedy for the advance of our Trade, and the keeping our Coin at Home, and enlargeth much upon it in his Appendix, which is To diminish the intrinsick value of our Coin.

If the Gentleman had understood Trade half so well, as he is said to do Mortgages, Bonds and Bills, certainly he would not have mentioned this old thred-bare and exploded Project, which is a trick hath been tried so often in Spain, till it hath left them more black Money (as they call it) then white or yellow, notwithstanding their Silver Mines in Peru and Mexico, and that their Laws make it Death to export Gold or Silver.

This Conceit I have known three times experienced likewise in Portugal, within this 24 or 25 years, at first the piece of 8 Rials went at 400 Ries, after that was brought to 480, after that to 520, and now to 600 Ries, and yet still we bring their Money from them as heretofore, and sell our Commodities to them for as much Silver as ever.

The reason is evident; suppose for example, a Hat that was usually sold to them for 4 pieces of 8, when the piece of 8 was at 400 Ries, we then sold such a Hat for 1600 Ries, when they raised the piece of eight 80 Ries per piece more, we sold the same Hat at 2000 Ries, and so rising in proportion as they raised their Coin, the Merchant still observing what the intrinsick value of the Money is, not the name it is called by, and so it would be in England, or any part of the World.

I have now done with all I can find of novelty in this Gentlemans Treatise; to meddle with old and stale matter, which in other words hath been often said, and as often answered, would be but to trouble the Reader with Impertinencies; so would it likewise to use opprobrious, calumniating Reflections, as he doth covertly in a business of that seriousness, weight and publick concernment as this is; I understand not the World so little as not to know, that he that will faithfully serve his Country, must be content to pass through good Report and evil Report, neither regard I which I meet with, Truth I am sure at last will vindicate it self, and be found by my Country-men.

Yet before I conclude this Preface, I must needs take notice of one thing to be wondred at, viz. That some had the Confidence publickly to assert before the Lords, when this Controversie was debated before their Lordships; that when Interest was at 10 per cent, Land was sold at 20 years Purchase; a strange, presumptious and incredible Assertion against Records, against Experience, and against Reason; to which I doubt not but their Lordships will be able to give a full confutation out of their own Memorials, before this be made publick.

And for the Reason of it, will any Man believe that our Fathers were so stupid, as to lay out their Money in Land, not to see it again in twenty years, when at single Interest at ten per cent they might double their Money in 10 years, at Interest upon Interest in seven years?

I have been told by a person of very great Honour, that this Gentleman himself in his private discourse, confesseth, that the Abatement of Interest will advance the value of Land; but he questions whether it will encrease Trade; certainly a needless scruple to any Man that shall deliberately consider the inseperable affinity that is in all Nations, and at all times between Land and Trade, which are Twins, and have always, and ever will wax and wane together, It cannot be ill with Trade, but Land will fall, nor ill with Lands, but Trade will feel it.

But in regard this Gentleman is so miserably mistaken in

the Trades of Spain and Portugal, which he reckons as lost; I think it may be useful to inform him, and others better, what Trades are really lost, and enquire how we came to loose them? and what Trades we still retain, and why, and of both as briefly as I can? because I have said something of them in the following Treatise.

Of Trades lost.

1. The Russia Trade, where the Dutch had last year 22 Sail of great Ships, and the Engilsh but one, whereas formerly we had more of that Trade then the Dutch.

2. The Green-land Trade, where the Dutch and Hamburgers have yearly at least 4 or 500 Sail of Ships, and the English but one the last year, and none the former.

3. The great Trade of Salt from St Vuals in Portugal, and from France, with Salt, Wine and Brandy to the East-lands.

4. All that vast and notorious Trade of Fishing for white-Herrings upon our own Coast.

5. The East-Country Trade, in which we have not half so much to do as we had formerly, and the Dutch ten times more then they had in times past.

6. A very great part of our Trade for Spanish-Woolls from Bilvao. These Trades and some more I could name, the Dutch Interest of 3 per cent, and narrow limitted Companies in England have beat us out of.

7. The East-India Trade for Nutmegs, Cloves and Mace, (an extraordinary profitable Trade) the Dutch Arms and Sleights have beat us out of; but their lower Interest gave strength to their Arms, and acuteness to their Invention.

8. Their great Trade for China and Japan, (whereof we have no share) is an effect of their low Interest, those Trades not being to be obtained but by a long process, and great disburstments,

destitute of present, but with expectation of future Gain, which 6 per cent cannot bear.

9. The Trades of Scotland and Ireland, two of our own Kingdoms, the Dutch have bereaved us of, and in effect wholly engrossed to themselves; which their low Interest hath been the principal engine, though I know other accidents have contributed thereunto, whereof more hereafter.

10. The Trade for Norway is in great part lost to the Danes, Holsteners, &c. by reason of some clauses in the Act of Navigation, whereof more in due place.

11. A very great part of the French Trade for Exportation is lost, by reason of great Impositions laid there upon our Draperies.

12. A great part of the Plate-Trade from Cadiz is lost to the Dutch, who by reason of the lowness of their Interest, can afford to let their Stocks lie before-hand at Civil and Cadiz, against the arrival of the Spanish Flota, who sometimes are expected 3, 6, 9, and 12 Months before they come, especially since the late interruptions that our Jamaica Capers have given them; by which means they engross the greatest part of the Silver, whereas we, in regard our Stocks run at a higher Interest, cannot so well afford to keep them so long dead. It is true, the English have yet a share in this Trade, by reason of some after recited natural advantages, viz. Woollen-Manufactures, Tin, Lead, Fish, &c. inseparably annexed by God's Providence to this Kingdom. It is true likewise, that the Peace at Munster hath much furthered the Dutch in that affair; but as true it is, that their lower Interest hath enabled them to make a much greater improvement and advantage in Trade by that Peace, then ever they could otherwise have done.

13. The Trade of Surranham, since the Dutch got possession of that Country in the late War, is so totally lost to the English,

that we have now no more Commerce with that Country, then we should have if it were sunk in the Sea; so severe and exact are the Hollanders, in keeping the Trades of their own Plantations intirely to their own People

14. The trade of Menades or New-York, we should have gained instead of the former, since we got possession of that place in the late War, if the Dutch had not bin connived at therein at first, which now I hope they are not; for if they should be, it would not only be to the intire loss of that Trade to England, but greatly to the prejudice of the English trade to Virginia, because the Dutch, under pretence of trading to and from New-York, carry great quantities of Virginia Tobacco directly for Holland.

15. The English Trade to Guiny I fear is much declined, by reason that Company have met with Discouragements from some of our Neighbours.

Note, That most of the afore-mentioned Trades are the greatest Trades in the World, for the employment of Shiping and Sea-men.

2dly, That no Trades deserve so much care to procrue, and preserve, and encouragement to prosecute, as those that employ the most Shiping, although the Commoditities transported be of small value in themselves; For, first, they are certainly the most profitable; for besides the gain accrewing by the Goods, the Freight, which is in such Trades often more then the value of the Goods, is all profit to the Nation; besides, they bring with them a great access of Power (Hands as well as Money) many Ships and Seamen being justly the reputed Strength and Safety of England.

I could mention more Trades that we have lost, and are in the High-way to loose, but I shall forbear at present, for fear this Porch should prove too big, as also for other Reasons.

The Trades we yet retain are;

1st, For Fish, the Trade of Red-Herrings at Yarmouth, Pilchards in the West-Country, and Cod-fish in New-found-land and New-England.

2dly, A good part of the Turkey, Italian, Spanish and Portugal Trades.

Our Trades to and from our own Plantations, viz. Virginia, Barbadoes, New-England, Jamaica, and the Leward Islands.

If any shall here ask me, How it comes to pass that the Dutch low Interest hath not cashered us of these Trades, as well as the former? I shall answer, first generally, and then particularly.

1. Generally I say, the Dutch low Interest hath miserably lessend us in all Trades of the World, not secured to us by Laws, or by some natural advantage which over-ballanceth the disproportion of our Interest of Money, which disproportion I take to be 3 per cent.

2. Particularly the Red-Herring Trade we retain, by reason of two natural Advantages, one is, the Fish for that purpose must be brought fresh on Shore, and that the Dutch cannot do with theirs, because the Herrings swim on our Coast, and consequently at too great a distance from theirs.

The other is, those Herrings must be smoked with Wood, which cannot be done on any reasonable terms, but in a woody Country, such as England is, and Holland is not. These advantages that God hath given our Land do counterpoize, and overpoize the disproportion of Interest, viz. 3 per Cent, otherwise we might say, Farewel Red-Herring as well as White.

The Pilchards on the West-Coast likewise come to our Shores, and must be cured and pressed upon the Land, which is impossible for the Dutch to do.

The New-found-land Fishing is managed by West-Country-men, whose Ports are properly scituated for that Country, and the Country it self is his Majesty's; so the Dutch can have no footing there, if they could, 3 per Cent would soon send us home to keep Sheep.

As to the Turkey, Italian, Spanish and Portugal Trades, though our vent for fine Cloth, and some sorts of Stuffs be declined, yet we retain a very considerable part of those Trades, by reason of some Natural, and some Artificial or Legal Advantages, which preponderates 3 per cent, such as these:

1st, The Wool of which our midling and course Clothes are made of, is our own, and consequently cheaper to us then the Dutch can steal it from us, paying Freights, Commission, Bribes and Cousenage, and sometimes armed Guards to force it off.

2dly, Our Fewel and Victual is cheaper in remote parts from London, and consequently our Manufacturers can and do work cheaper then the Dutch, whatever Mr Manley erroneously affirms.

3dly, The Red-Herring, Pilchard, New-found-land and New-England Fishery, by which we carry on much of those Trades, are inseparably annexed to this Kingdom, as before is demonstrated, and by the bounty of God Almighty, not by our own Wisdom or Industry.

4thly, Our Lead and Tin by which we carry on much of those Trades, are Natives with us.

5thly, Our Country consumes within it self more of Spanish Wines and Fruit, Zant Currans and Levant Oyls, then any Country in Europe.

6thly, Which is an artificial advantage (and due to the wisdom of the Contrivers) our Act of Navigation compels us, or at least would do, if it were justly administred, to import none of those Goods but from the proper Ports of their Imbarkation, and by English Shiping only.

The Trades to and from all our own Plantations, are likewise secured to us by the Act of Navigation, or would be, if that Act were truly executed, and if it were not for that, you should see forty Dutch Ships at our own Plantations for one English.

To conclude this paragraph, the Dutch low Interest, through our own supineness, hath robbed us totally of all Trade, not inseperably annexed to this Kingdom by the benevolence of divine Providence, and our Act of Navigation, which, though it have some things in it wanting amendment, deserves to be called our (Charta Maritima) insomuch as with shame to our selves, it may be truly said of us, as we Proverbially say to careless Persons, They have lost all that is loose.

When I think of these things, I cannot but wonder that there should be found English men who want not Bread to eat, or Clothes to wear, should be yet so unkind and hardhearted to their Country, as strenuously to endeavour (for private Ends) the depriving her of so great a good, as would be the abatement of our Interest to 4 per Cent, by a Law. I have lately seen a Treatise writ about thirty Years since, by Lewis Roberts, Merchant, wherein he highly exaggerates (and with great Reason) the wonderful advantage the Dutch have by the lowness of their Customs, but seeing an exact imitation in that respect is not consistant with our Affairs at present, though much to be desired in due time. I insist not thereupon, but think it necessary by the way, to make this true Animadversion, viz. That 2 per Cent. extraordinary in Interest is worse then 4 per Cent. extraordinary in Customs, because Customs run only upon our Goods imported or exported, and that but once for all; whereas Interest runs as well upon our Ships, as Goods, and must be yearly paid on both so long as they are in being, and the Ships in many bulkey Trades, and such as are Nationally most profitable, are of four times the value of the Goods.

That old Objection about Widows and Orphans, I have I think fully answered in my former Treatise, but because I yet sometimes meet with it, I shall say a Word more to it here, viz.

1. Widows and Orphans are not one to twenty of the whole

People; and its the Wisdom of Law-makers to provide for the good of the Majority of People, though a Minor part should a little suffer.

2. Of Widows and Orphans, not one in forty will suffer by the abatement of Interest for these Reasons, viz.

1st. Of Widows and Orphans nine of ten in this Kingdom have very little or nothing at all left them by their deceased Relations, and all such will have an advantage by the abatement of Interest, because such abatement will encrease Trade, and in consequence occasion more employment for such necessitous Persons.

2dly, Many Widows and Orphans have Joyntures, Annuities, Coppy-Holds, and other Lands left them, as well as Money; and all such will be gainers by the abatement of Interest.

3dly, For all London Orphans the City gives not now above 5, and to some 4 per cent. Interest, so the loss to such is not worth speaking of.

4thly, Many Executors are so unworthy as to allow Orphans no Interest, and yet justifie themselves by Law; to such Orphans it will be all one what the legal rate of Interest be.

5thly, When the Law for abatement of Interest is past, many more Parents will leave their Children Annuities and Estates running in Trade, as they do in Holland and Italy, whereby the abatement of Interest will become profitable, not prejudicial to them.

And for the few that at first may happen to suffer, whereof the number will be very small (and therefore not to be named in competition with the common good of the Kingdom) they have an easie means within their own Power, to prevent their being one Farthing the worse for the abatement of Interest; it is but wearing a Lawn-Whisk instead of a Point de Venice; and for the meaner sort a Searge Petty-Coat, instead of a Silk one, and a plain pair of Shoes instead of laced ones. And that the

Ladies may not be offended with me, I dare undertake that this will never spoil, but mend their Marriages; besides the greater good it will bring to their Country, and to their Posterities after them, whether they prove to be Noblemen, Gentlemen or Merchants, &c.

I have in several places of my ensuing Treatise, referred to some Tracts I formerly published upon this subject, which being now wholly out of Print, I thought fit to Re-print and annex unto this, which at first I intended not.

Some there are who would grant that abatement of Interest, if it could be effected, would procure to the Nation all the good that I alledge it will bring with it, but say it is not practicable, or at least not now.

1. A needless scruple, and contradictory to experience, for first, a Law hath abated Interest in England, three times within these few Years already; and what should hinder its effect now more then formerly?

2. If a Law will not do it, why do the Usurers raise such a dust, and engage so many Friends to oppose the passing of an Act to this purpose?

The true reason is, because they are wise enough to know that a Law will certainly do it, as it hath done already, though they would perswade others the contrary. And if it be doubted we have not Money enough in England. Besides what I have said in my former Treatise as to the encrease of our Riches in general, I shall here give some further Reasons of probability, which are the best that can be expected in this case, to prove that we have now much more Money in England then we had twenty Years past.

Notwithstanding the seeming scarcity at present, if I should look further back then twenty years, the argument would be stronger on my side, and the proportion of the encrease of Money greater, and more perspicuous; but I shall confine my self to that time which is within most mens Memories.

1. We give generally now one third more Money with Apprentices then we did twenty years past.

2. Notwithstanding the decay and loss of sundry Trades and Manufactures, yet in the gross we Ship off now one third part more of the Manufactures, as also Lead and Tin, then we did twenty years past, which is a cause, as well as a proof of our increase of Money.

If any doubt this, if they please to consult Mr Dickins, Surveyor of his Majesties Customs, who is the best able I know living, and hath taken the most pains in these Calculations, he may be satisfactorily resolved.

3. Houses new built in London yield twice the Rent they did before the Fire; and Houses generally immediately before the Fire yielded about one fourth part more Rent then they did twenty years past.

4. The speedy and costly buildings of London is a convincing (and to Strangers an amazing) Argument of the plenty, and late encrease of Money in England.

5. We have now more then double the quantity of Merchants Shiping we had twenty years past.

6. The course of our Trade from the increase of our Money is strangely altered within these twenty years, most Payments from Merchants and Shop-keepers being now made with ready Money, whereas formerly the course of our general Trade run at three, six, nine, twelve and eighteen Months time.

But if this case be so clear, some may ask me, How comes it to pass that all sorts of men complain so much of the scarcity of Money, especially in the Country?

My answers to this Query are, viz.

1. This proceeds from the Frailty and Corruption of humane Nature, it being natural for men to complain of the present, and commend the times past; so said they of Old, The former

days were better then these; and I can say in truth, upon my own Memory, that men did complain as much of the scarcity of Money, ever since I knew the world as they do now; nay, the very same Persons that now complain of this, and commend that time.

2. And more particularly, This complaint proceeds from many mens finding themselves uneasie in the matters of their Religion, it being natural for men, when they are discontented at one thing, to complain of all, and principally to utter their discontents and complaints in those things which are most popular. Those that hate a man for some one cause, will seldom allow of any thing that is good in him; and some that are angry with one person, or thing, will find fault with others that gave them no offence; like peevish Persons that meeting discontent abroad, coming home, quarrel with their Wifes, Children, Servants, &c.

3. And more especially this complaint in the Country, proceeds from the late practice of bringing up the Tax-Money in Wagons to London, which did doubtless cause a scarcity of Money in the Country.

4. And principally this seeming scarcity of Money proceeds from the Trade of Bankering, which obstructs circulation, advanceth Usury, and renders it so easie, that most Men as soon as they can make up a Sum of 50 l. or a 100 l. send it into the Gold-Smith; Which doth, and will occasion while it lasts, that fatal pressing necessity for Money, so visible throughout the whole Kingdom, both to Prince and People.

From what hath been last said, it appears the matter in England is prepared for the abatement of Interest which as Sr Henry Blunt, (an honourable Member of his Majesties Council of Trade) well said before the Lords at the debate, is the Unum Magnum towards the prosperity of this Kingdom: It is a generative good, and will bring many other good things with it.

I shall conclude with two or three Requests to the Reader.

1. That he would Read, and consider what he Reads, with an entire Love to his Country, void of private interests, and former ill grounded impressions received into his mind, to the prejudice of this principle.

2. That he would Read all (minding the matter, not the stile) before he make a judgment.

3. That in all his meditations upon these Principles, he would warily distinguish between the Profit of the Merchant and the Gain of the Kingdom, which are so far from being always parallels, that frequently they run counter one to the other, although most Men by their Education and Business, having fixed their eye and aim wholly upon the former, do usually confound these two in their Thoughts and Discourses of Trade, or else mistake the former for the latter; from which false measures have proceeded, many vulgar errors in Trade, some whereof by reason of Mens frequent mistakings, as aforesaid, are become almost Proverbial, and often heard out of the Mouths, not only of the common People, but of Men that might know better, if they would duly consider the afore-said distinction.

Some of the said common Proverbial errors are, viz.

1. Vulgar Error; We have too many Merchants already.

2. The Stock of England is too big for the Trade of England.

3. No Man should exercise two Callings.

4. Especially no Shop-keeper ought to be a Merchant.

5. Luxury and some Excess may be profitable.

6. We have people enough, and more then we can employ.

7. To suffer Artificers to have as many Apprentices as they will, is to destroy Trade.

8. The admission of Strangers is to call in others to eat the Bread out of our own Mouthes.

9. No man ought to Live and Trade in a Corporation, that is

not a Free-man of the place.

10. Nor should any be Free-men, that are not the sons of Free-men, or have served seven years Apprentiship.

11. Its better we Trade but for a hundred pound at 20 per cent. profit, then for three hundred at 10 per cent. profit, and so pro rata.

12. Our Plantations depopulate, and consequently impoverish England; with abundance more that might be named, but that many of them are occasionally hinted, and I hope them and others confuted in the following Discourse.

By what hath been said, and what follows, as well as by what most Men observe; It is evident that this Kingdom is wonderfully fitted by the bounty of God Almighty for a great Progression in Wealth and Power; and that the only means to arrive at both or either of them, is to improve and advance Trade; and that the way to those Improvements is not hedged up with thorns, nor hidden from us in the dark, or intrigued with difficulties, but very natural and facile, if we would set about them, and begin the right way, casting off some of our old mistaken Principles in Trade, which we inherit from our Ancestors, who were Souldiers, Hunts-men, and Herds-men, and therefore necessarily unskilful in the Mysteries of, and Methods to improve Trade (though their natural Parts were nothing inferiour to ours) Trade being but a novel thing in England, comparatively to other parts of the World; and in my opinion not yet advanced to the one fifth part of improvement that this Land is capable of, and I think no true English-man will deny that the season cries aloud to us to be up and doing, before our Fields become unoccupied, and before the Dutch get too much the whip-hand of us, whom (in such a case were they freed from their French fears which they labour under at present) I fear we should find as severe task-Masters, as ever the Athenians were to the lesser Trading Cities of Greece.

Neither are the Dutch the only Neighbours we have at this time for corrivals in Trade, but the French King and King of Sweeden are now as active, circumspect, industrious and prospective too in this Affair; and have, and are ordering things as prudently for promoting thereof, as the Dutch themselves.

When I began to Write this Treatise, I intended not to enlarge upon so many particulars, and the rather because nothing can be said for publick good, but will cross the particular ends, as well as the opinions of many private persons, and still the more is said, the more are disobliged, but my Duty to my Country overcoming those doubtful Considerations, I have adventured this second time to expose my Conceptions to publick censure, with this confidence, that after these Principles have suffered the accustomary Persecution of Tongues and Pens, naturally and constantly accompanying all new Proposals for a while, they will at length the most, if not all of them, or something very like them, come to be generally received and honoured with the publick Sanction, by being passed into Laws (gradually not at once) concerning the time whereof I am not careful, but for my Countries sake, I could wish it might be shortened.

A DISCOURSE ABOUT TRADE

THE CONTENTS

A DISCOURSE ABOUT TRADE

THE CONTENTS

A DISCOURSE ABOUT TRADE

A DISCOURSE CONCERNING TRADE

A DISCOURSE ABOUT TRADE

A DISCOURSE CONCERNING TRADE

The Prodigious increase of the Netherlanders in their Domestick and Foreign Trade, Riches, and multitude of Shipping, is the Envy of the present, and may be the wonder of all future Generations: And yet the means whereby they have thus advanced themselves, are sufficiently obvious, and in a great measure imitable by most other Nations, but more easily by us of this Kingdom of England, which I shall endeavour to demonstrate in the following Discourse.

Some of the said means by which they have advanced their Trade, and thereby improved their Estates are these following.

First, They have in their greatest Councils of State and War, Trading-Merchants that have lived abroad in most parts of the World; who have not only the Theoretical Knowledge, but the practical Experience of Trade, by whom Laws and Orders are contrived, and Peaces with foreign Princes projected, to the great Advantage of their Trade.

Secondly, Their Law of Gavel-kind, whereby all their Children possess an equal share of their Fathers Estates after their decease, and so are not left to wrastle with the World in their youth, with inconsiderable assistance of Fortune, as most of our youngest Sons of Gentlemen in England are, who are bound Apprentices to Merchants.

Thirdly, Their exact making of all their Native Commodities, and packing of their Herrings, Codfish, and all other Commodities, which they send abroad in great quantities; the consequence whereof is, That the repute of their said Commodities abroad, continues always good, and the Buyers will accept of them by the Marks, without opening; whereas the Fish which our English make in New-found-Land and New-England, and Herrings at Yarmouth, often prove false and deceitfully made; and our Pilchards from the West-Country false packed, seldom containing the quantity for which the Hogsheads are marked in which they are packed.

And in England the attempts which our Fore-fathers made for Regulating of Manufactures, when left to the Execution of some particular person, in a short time resolved but into a Tax upon the Commodity, without respect to the goodness thereof; as most notoriously appears in the business of the AULNAGE, which doubtless our Predecessors intended for a scrutiny into the goodness of the Commodity; and to that purpose a Seal was invented, as a signal that the Commodity was made according to the Statutes, which Seals it is said, may now be bought by Thousands, and put upon what the Buyers please.

Fourthly, Their giving great incouragement and immunities to the Inventors of New Manufactures, and the Discoverers of any New Mysteries in Trade, and to those that shall bring the Commodities of other Nations first in use and practice amongst them; for which the Author never goes without his due Reward allowed him at the Publick Charge.

Fifthly, Their Contriving and Building of great Ships to sail with small charge, not above one third of what we are at, for Ships of the same Burthen in England; and compelling their said Ships (being of small Force) to sail always in Fleets, to which in all time of danger they allow Convoy.

Sixthly, Their parcimonious and thrifty Living, which is so extraordinary, that a Merchant of One hundred thousand Pound Estate with them, will scarce spend so much per annum, as one of Fifteen hundred Pounds Estate in London.

Seventhly, The Education of their Children, as well Daughters as Sons; all which, be they of never so great Quality or Estate, they always take care to bring up to write perfect good Hands, and to have the full knowledge and use of Arithemetick and Merchants-Accounts; the well understanding and practice whereof, doth strangely infuse into most that are the owners of that Quality, of either Sex, not only an Ability for Commerce of all kinds, but a strong aptitude, love and delight in it; and in regard the Women are as knowing therein as the Men, it doth incourage their Husbands to hold on in their Trades to their dying days, knowing the capacity of their Wives to get in their Estates, and carry on their Trades after their Deaths: Whereas if a Merchant in England arrive at any considerable Estate, he commonly with-draws his Estate from Trade, before he comes near the confines of old Age; reckoning that if God should call him out of the World, while the main of his Estate is engaged abroad in Trade, he must lose one third of it, through the unexperience and unaptness of his Wife to such Affairs, and so it usually falls out.

Besides, it hath been observed in the nature of Arithmetick, that like other parts of the Mathematicks, it doth not only improve the Rational Faculties, but inclines those that are expert in it to Thriftiness and good-Husbandry, and prevents both Husbands and Wives in some measure from running out of their Estates, when they have it always ready in their Heads what their Expences do amount to, and how soon by that course their Ruin must overtake them.

Eightly, The lowness of their Customs, and the height of

their Excise, which is certainly the most equal and indifferent Tax in the World, and least prejudical to any people, as might be made appear, were it the subject of this Discourse.

Ninthly, The careful providing for, and employment of their Poor, which it is easie to demonstrate can never be done in England comparatively to what it is with them, while it's left to the care of every Parish to look after their own only.

Tenthly, Their use of BANKS, which are of so immence advantage to them, that some not without good grounds have estimated the Profit of them to the Publick, to amount to at least one Million of Pounds sterling per annum.

Eleventhly, Their Toleration of different Opinions in matters of Religion: by reason whereof many industrious People of other Countries, that dissent from the Established Government of their own Churches, resort to them with thetr Families and Estates, and after a few years co-habitation with them, become of the same Common interest.

Twelfthly, Their Law-Merchant, By which all Controversies between Merchants and Tradesmen are decided in three or four days time, and that not at the fortieth part (I might say in many cases not the hundredth part) of the charge they are with us.

Thirteenthly, The Law that is in use among them for Transferrence of Bills for Debt from one Man to another: This is of extraordinary advantage to them in their Commerce; by means whereof, they can turn their Stocks twice or thrice in Trade, for once that we can in England; for that having sold our Foreign Goods here, we cannot buy again to advantage, till we are possest of our Money; which it may be we shall be six, nine, or twelve Months in recovering: And if what we sell be considerable, it is a good Man's work all the Year to be following Vintners and Shop-keepers for Money. Whereas, were the Law for Transferring Bills in practice with us, we could presently after sale of our Goods, dispose of our Bills, and close up our Accounts. To do which, the Advantage, ease, and Accommodations it would be to Trade, is so great, that none but Merchants that have lived where that custom is in use, can value to its due proportion.

Fourteenthly, Their keeping up PUBLICK REGISTERS of all Lands and Houses, Sold or Mortgaged, whereby many chargable Law-Suits are prevented, and the securities of Lands and Houses rendred indeed, such as we commonly call them, REAL SECURITIES.

Lastly, The lowness of Interest of Money with them, which in peaceable times exceeds not three per cent per annum; and is now during this War with England, not above four per cent at most.

Some more Particulars might be added, and those aforesaid further improved, were it my purpose to discourse at large of Trade. But seeing most of the former Particulars are observed and granted by all men that make it any part of their business, to inspect the true nature and Principles of Trade; but the last is not so much as taken notice of by the most Ingenious, to be any Cause of the great encrease of the Riches and Commerce of that people.

I shall therefore in this Paper confine my self to write principally my Observations touching that, viz.

The Profit That People have received, and any other may receive, by reducing the Interest of Money to a very low rate.

This in my poor opinion, is the Causa Causans of all the other causes of the Riches of that People; and that if Interest of Money were with us reduced to the same rate it is with them, i would in a short time render us as rich and considerable in Trade as they now are, and consequently be of greater damage to them, and advantage to us, then can happen by the Issue of this present War, though the success of it should be as good as we can wish, except it end in their total Ruin and Extirpation.

To illustrate this, let us Impartially search our Books, and enquire what the state and condition of this Kingdom was, as to Trade and Riches, before any Law concerning Interest of Money was made: The first whereof that I can find, was Anno 1545. and we shall be informed that the Trade of England then was Inconsiderable, and the Merchants very mean and few: And that afterwards, viz. Anno 1635. within ten Years after Interest was brought down to eight per Cent, there was more Merchants to be found upon the Exchange worth each One Thousand Pounds and upwards, then were in the former dayes, viz. before the Year 1600. to be found worth One Hundred Pounds each.

And now since Interest hath been for about twenty Years at six per Cent, notwithstanding our long civil Wars, and the great complaints of the deadness of Trade, there are more men to be found upon the Exchange now worth Ten thousand Pounds Estates, then were then of One thousand Pounds.

And if this be doubted, let us ask the aged, whether five hundred pounds Portion with a Daughter sixty Years ago, were not esteemed a larger proportion then Two thousand pounds is now: And whether Gentlewomen in those dayes would not esteem themselves well cloathed in a Searge Gown, which a Chamber-Maid now will be ashamed to be seen in: Whether our Citizens and middle sort of Gentry now are not more rich in Cloaths, Plate, Jewels, and Houshold-Goods, &c. then the best sort of Knights and Gentry were in those days. And whether our best sort of Knights and Gentry now do not exceed by much in those things the Nobility of England sixty Years past: Many of whom then would not go to the price of a whole Sattin-Doublet; the Embroiderer being yet living, who hath assured me he hath made many hundreds of them for the Nobility with Canvas backs.

Which way ever we take our measures, to me it seems

evident, that since our first abatement of Interest, the Riches and Splendor of this Kingdom is increased to above four (I might say above six) times so much as it was.

We have now almost One hundred Coaches for one we had formerly. We with case can pay a greater Tax now in one Year, then our Fore-fathers could in twenty.

Our Customs are very much improved, I believe above the proportion aforesaid, of six to one, which is not so much in advance of the Rates of Goods, as by encrease of the bulk of Trade; for though some Foreign Commodities are advanced, others of our Native Commodities and Manufactures are considerably abated, by the last Book of Rates.

I can my self remember since there were not in London used so many Wharfs or Keys for the Landing of Merchants Goods, by at least one third part as now there are; and those that were then, could scarce have Imployment for half what they could do; and now notwithstanding one third more used to the same purpose, they are all too little in a time of Peace, to land the Goods at, that come to London.

If we look into the Country, we shall find Lands as much Improved since the abatement of Interest, as Trade, &c. in Cities; that now yielding twenty Years purchase, which then would not have sold for above eight or ten at most

Besides, the Rent of Farms have been for these last thirty Years much advanced; and although they have for these three or four last years fallen, that hath no respect at all to the lowness of Interest at present, nor to the other mistaken Reasons which are commonly assigned for it.

But principally to the vast Improvement of Ireland, since a great part of it was lately possessed by the Industrous English, who were Soldiers in the late Army, and the late great Land-Taxes.

More might be said, but the Premises being considered, I

judge will sufficiently demonstrate how greatly this Kingdom of England hath been advanc'd in all respects for these last fifty Years: And that the abatement of Interest hath been the cause thereof, to me seems most probable; because as it appears, it hath been in England, so I find it is at this day in all Europe, and other parts of the World: Insomuch that to know whether any Country be rich or poor, or in what proportion it is so, no other Question needs to be resolved, but this, viz. What Interest do they pay for Money? Near home we see it evidently, in Scotland and Ireland, where ten and twelve per Cent is paid for Interest, the People are poor and despicable, their Persons ill cloathed, their Houses worse provided, and Money intollerably scarce, notwithstanding they have great plenty of all Provisions, nor will their Land yield above eight or ten Years purchase at most.

In France where Money is at seven per Cent, their Lands will yield about eighteen Years purchase; and the Gentry who may possess Lands, live in good condition, though the Peasants are little better then Slaves, because they can possess nothing but at the will of others.

In Italy Money will not yield above three per Cent, to be let out upon real Security, there the People are rich, full of Trade, well attired, and their Lands will sell at thirty five to forty Years purchase; and that it is so, or better with them in Holland, is too manifest.

In Spain the usual Interest is ten and twelve per Cent, and there, notwithstanding they have the only Trade in the World for Gold and Silver, Money is no where more scarce; the people poor, despicable, and void of Commerce, other then such as English, Dutch, Italians, Jews, and other Foreigners bring to them; who are to them in effect, but as Leeches, who suck their Blood and vital Spirits from them.

I might urge many other Instances of this nature, not only

out of Christendom, but from under the Turks Dominions, East-India and America: But every man by his Eperience in Foreign Countries, may easiy inform himself, whether this Rule do universally hold true or not: For my own part, to satisfie my own curiosity, I have for some Years, as occasion offered, diligently enquired of all my acquaintance that had knowledge of foreign Countries, and I can truly say that I never found it to fail in any particular Instance.

Now if upon what hath been said, it be granted that defacto, this Kingdom be richer at least four-fold, (I might say eight-fold) then it was before any Law for Interest was made, and that all Countries are at this day richer or poorer in an exact proportion to what they pay, and have usually paid for the Interest of Money; it remains that we enquire carefully, whether the abatement of Interest be in truth the Cause of the Riches of any Country, or only the Concomitant or Effect of the Riches of a Country; in which seems to lie the Intricacy of this Question.

To satisfie my self wherein, I have taken all opportunities to discourse this point, with the most ingenious men I had the Honour to be known to, and have searcht for, and read all the Books that I could ever hear were printed against the Abatement of Interest, and seriously considered all the Arguments and Objections used by them against it: All which have tended to confirm me in this opinion, which I bumbly offer to the consideration of wiser Heads, viz. That the Abatement of Interest is the Cause of the Prosperity & Riches of any Nation, and that the bringing down of Interest in this Kingdom from six to four, or three per Cent, will necessarily, in less then twenty Years time, double the Capital Stock of the Nation.

The most material Objections I have met with against it, are as follows:

Object. 1. To abate Interest, will cause the Dutch, and

other People that have Money put out at Interest in England, by their Friends and Factors, to call home their Estates, and consequently will occasion a great scarcity and want of Money amongst us.

To this I answer, That if Interest be brought but to four per Cent, no Dutchman will call in his Money that is out upon good Security in England, because he cannot make above three per Cent of it upon Interest at home. But if they should call home all the Money they have with us at Interest, it would be better for us than if they did it not; for the Borrower is alwayes a slave to the Lender, and shall be sure to be always kept poor, while the other is fat and full: HE THAT USETH A STOCK THAT IS NONE OF HIS OWN, BEING FORCED FOR THE UPHOLDING HIS REPUTATION TO LIVE TO THE FULL, IF NOT ABOVE THE PROPORTION OF WHAT HE DOTH SO USE, WHILE THE LENDER POSSESING MUCH, AND USING LITTLE OR NONE, LIVE ONLY AT THE CHARGE OF WHAT HE USETH, AND NOT OF WHAT HE HATH

Besides, if with this Law for abatement of Interest, a Law for Transferring Bills of Debt should pass, we should not miss the Dutch Money, were it ten times as much as it is amongst us; for that such a Law will certainly supply the the defect of at least one half of all the ready Money we have in use in the Nation.

Object. 2. If Interest be abated, Land must rise in purchase, and consequently Rents; and if Rents, then the Fruits of the Land; and so all things will be dear, and how shall the Poor live? &c.

Answ. To this I say, If it follow that the Fruits of our Land, in consequence of such a Law for abatement of Interest, grow generally dear, it is an evident demonstration that our People grow richer; for generally, where-ever Provisions are for continuance of Years dear in any Country, the People are rich;

and where they are most cheap throughout the World, for the most part the People are very poor.

And for our own Poor in England, it is observed, That they live better in the dearest Countries for Provisions, than in the cheapest, and better in a dear year than in a cheap, (especially in relation to the publick good) for that in a cheap Year they will not work above two dayes in a Week; their humour being such, that they will not provide for a hard time; but just work so much and no more, as may maintain them in that mean condition to which they have been accustomed.

Object. 3. If Interest be abated, Usurers will call in their Money; so what shall Gentlemen do, whose Estates are Mortgaged? &c.

Answ. I answer, That when they know they can make no more of their Money by taking out of one, and putting it in another hand, they will not be so forward as they threaten, to alter that Security they know is good, for another that may be bad: Or if they should do it, our Laws are not so severe, but that Gentlemen may take time to dispose of part of their Land, which immediately after such a Law will yield them thirty years purchase at least, and much better it is for them so to do, than to abide longer under that consuming Plague of Usury, which hath insensibly destroyed very many of the best Families in England, as well of our Nobility as Gentry.

Object. 4. As Interest is now at six per cent, the Kings Majesty upon any emergency can hardly be supplied; and if it should be reduced to four per cent, how shall the King find a considerable sum of Money to be lent him by his People?

Answ. I answer, The abatement of Interest to the People, is the abatement of Interest to the King, when he hath occasion to take up Money: For what is borrowed of the City of London, or other Bodies Politick, nothing can be demanded but the legal Interest; and if the King have occasion to take up Money of private Persons, being his Majesty, according to good right, is above the common course of Law, the King must, and always hath given more then the legal Rate. As for instance: The legal Rate is now six per cent, but his Majesty, or such as have disposed of his Majesties Exchequer-Tallies, have been said to give ten and twelve in some cases; and if the legal Rate were ten, his Majesty might probably give thirteen or fourteen: So if Interest be brought to four per cent, his Majesty in such cases as he now gives ten, must give six or seven; by which his Majesty would have a clear advantage.

Object. 5. If Interest be abated, it will be a great prejudice to Widows and Orphans, who have not Knowledge and Abilities to improve their Estates otherwise.

Answ. I answer, That by our Law now, Heirs and Orphans can recover no Interest from their Parents Executors, except it be left fully and absolutely to the Executors to dispose and put out Money at the discretion of the Executors, for the profit and loss of the Heirs and Orphans: And if it be so left to the Executors discretion, they may improve the Monies left them in Trade, or purchase of Lands and Leases, as well as by Interest: Or when not, the damage such Heirs and Orphans will sustain in their minority, (being but two per cent) is inconsiderable, in respect of the great advantage will accrew to the Nation in generel, by such abatement of Interest.

Besides, when such a Law is made and in use, all Men will so take care in their Life to provide for, and educate their Children, and instruct their Wives, as that no prejudice can happen thereby; as we see there doth not in Holland and Italy, and other places where Interest is so low.

Having now offered my thoughts in answer to the aforesaid Objections, it will not be amiss, that we enquire who will be advantaged, and who will receive prejudice, in case such a Law be made.

First, His Majesty, as hath been said in answer to that Objection, will, when he hath occasion, take up Money on better terms: Besides which, He will receive a great Augmentation to his Revenue thereby, all his Lands being immediately worth, after the making such a Law, double to what they were before; his Customs will be much increas'd by the increase of Trade, which must necessarily insue upon the making such a Law.

The Nobility and Gentry, whose Estates he mostly in Land, may presently upon all they have, instead of Fifty, write one Hundred.

The Merchants and Tradesmen, who bear the Heat and Burthen of the Day, (most of our Trade being carried on by young Men that take up Money at Interest) will find their Yoak sit lighter upon their Shouldiers, and be incouraged to go on with greater alacrity in their Business.

Our Marriners, Shipwrights, Porters, Cloathiers, Packers, and all sorts of Labouring People that depend on Trade, will be more constantly and fully employed.

Our Farmers sell the product of their Lands at better rates. And whereas our Neighbours the Netherlanders (who in regard of the largeness of their Stocks, and Experiences, the Sons continually succeeding the Fathers in Trade to many Generations, we may not unfitly in this case term Sons of Anach, and Men of renown) against whom we fight Dwarfs and Pigmies in Stocks and Experience, being younger Brothers of Gentlemen that seldom have above one Thousand Pounds, sometimes not two Hundred to begin the World with: Instead I say of such young Men and small Stocks (if this Law pass) we shall bring forth out Sampsons and Goliahs in Stocks, subtilty, and experience in Trade to coap with our potent Adversaries on the other side; there being to every Mans knowledge that understands the Exchange of London, divers English Merchants of large Estates, which have not much past their middle-Age, and yet have wholly left off their Trades, having found the sweetness of Interest, which if that should abate, must again set their Hands to the Plough, (which they are as able to hold and govern now as ever) and also will engage them to train up their Sons in the same way, because it will not be so easie to make them Country-Gentlemen as now it is, when Lands sell at thirty or fourty years Purchase.

For the Sufferers by such a Law, I know none but idle Persons that lives at as little Expence as Labour, Neither scattering by their Expences, so as the Poor may Glean any thing after them, nor Working with their Hands or Heads to bring either Wax or Honey to the common Hive of the Kingdom; but swelling their own Purses by the sweat of other Mens Brows, and the contrivances of other Mens Brains: And how unprofitable it is for any Nation, to suffer Idleness to suck the Breasts of Industry; needs no Demonstration. And if it be granted me, that these will be the effects of an Abatement of Interest, then I think it is out of doubt, that the Abatement of Interest doth tend to the Enriching of a Nation, and consequently, hath been one great cause of the Riches of the Dutch and Italians, and the encrease of the Riches of our own Kingdom in these last fifty years.

Another Argument to prove which, we may draw from the nature of Interest it self, which is of so prodigious a Multiplying nature, that it must of necessity make the Lenders monstrous Rich, (if they live at any moderate Expence) and the Borrowers extream Poor: A memorial instance whereof, we have in Old Audley deceased, who did wisely observe, That one Hundred Pounds only, put out at Interest at ten per cent, doth in seventy years (which is but the Age of a Man) increase to above one Hundred Thousand Pounds: And if the Advantage be so great to the Lender, the Loss must be greater to the Borrower, who (as hath been said) lives at a much larger Expence. And as it is between private Persons, so between Nation and Nation, that have Communication one with another. For whether the Subjects of one Nation lend Money to Subjects of another, or Trade with them for Goods, the effect is the same. As for example, A Dutch Merchant that hath but four or five Thousand Pounds clear Stock of his own, can easily borrow and have credit for fifteen Thousand Pounds more at three per cent at Home; with which, whether he Trade or put it to Use in England, or any Country where Interest of Money is high, he must necessarily (without very evil Accidents attend him) in a very few years, treble his own Capital.

This discovers the true cause, why the Sugar-Bakers of Holland can afford to give a greater price for Barbadoes Sugars in London, besides the second Freight and Charges upon them between England and Holland, and yet grow exceeding Rich upon their Trade: Whereas our Sugar-Bakers in London, that buy Sugars here at their own Doors, before such additional Freight and Charges come upon them, can scarce live upon their Callings, ours here paying for a good share of their Stocks six per cent, and few of them employ in their Sugar-works, above six to ten Thousand Pounds at most: Whereas in Holland they employ twenty, thirty, to fourty Thousand Pounds Stock in a Sugar-House, paying but three per cent at most for what they take up at Interest, to fill up their said Stocks, which is sometimes half, sometimes three quarters of their whole Stocks. And as it is with this Trade, the same Rules holds throughout all other Trades whatsoever. And for us to say, if the Dutch put their Money to Interest among us, we shall have the advantage by being full and flush of Coin at Home; it is a mear Chymera, and so far from an Advantage, that it is an extream Loss, rendring us only in the condition of a young Gallant, that hath newly Mortgaged his Land, and with the Money thereby raised, stuffes his Pockets, and looks big for a time, not considering that the draught of Cordial he hath received, though it be at present grateful to his Pallat, doth indeed prey upon his vital Spirits; and will in a short time render the whole body of his Estate in a deep Consumption, if not wholly consumed: Besides, whatever Money the Dutch lends us, they always keep one end of the Chain at home in their own Hands; by which they can pull back when they please their Lean Kine which they send hither to be fatted.

This makes me conclude that Moses (that Wise Legislator) in his forbidding the Jews to lend Money at use one to another, and permitting them to lend their Money to Strangers, ordained that Law as much to a Political as a Religious intent; knowing that by the latter they should Enrich their own Nation, and by the former no publick Goods could insue; the consequence being only to Impoverish one Jew to make another Rich.

This likewise takes off the wonder how the People of Israel, out of so small a Territory as they possessed, could upon all occasions set forth such vast and numerous Armies (almost incredible) as all Histories, sacred and prophane, report they did; which is neither impossible nor strange to any that have well considered the effects of their Laws concrning Usury, which were sufficient to make any barren Land fruitful, and a fruitful Land an entire Garden, which by consequence would maintain ten times the number of Inhabitants that the same Tract of Land would do where no such Laws were.

To conclude, it is, (I think) agreed on by all, That Merchants, Artificers, Farmers of Land, and such as depend on them, (which for brevity-sake we may here include under one of these general terms) viz. Sea-men, Fisher-men, Breeders of Cattel, Gardners, &c. are the three sorts of People which by their Study and Labour do principally, if not only, bring in Wealth to a Nation from abroad; other kinds of People, viz. Nobility, Gentry, Lawyers, Physicians, Scholars of all sorts, and Shop-keepers, do only hand it from one to another at Home. And if abatement of Interest (besides the general Benefit it brings to all, except the Griping Dronish Usurer) will add new Life and Motion to those most profitable Engines of the Kingdom (as I humbly suppose) will be manifest upon serious consideration of what hath been said; then I think it will be out of doubt, that Abatement of Interest is the Cause of increase of the Trade and Riches of any Kingdom.

A DISCOURSE ABOUT TRADE

SUPPLIMENT

A DISCOURSE ABOUT TRADE

SUPPLIMENT

The fore-going Discourse I Wrote in the Sickness-Summer at my Country-Habitation, not then intending to publish it, but only to communicate it to some Honourable and Ingenious Friends of the present Parliament, who were pleased to take Copies of it for their own deliberate consideration and digestion of the Principles therein asserted; which at first were strange to them, as I expect they will be to most others, till they have spent some time in thinking on them; after which, I doubt not but all Men will be convinced of the Truth of them, that have not some private Interest of heir own against them, external to the general Good of the Kingdom. For sure I am they have a Foundation in Nature, and that according to the excellent, Sr William Petty's Observation in his late Discourse, concerning Taxes, Res nolune male Administrare: Nature must and will have its course, the matter in England is prepared for an Abatement of Interest, and it cannot long be obstructed, and after the next Abatement, who ever lives fourty Years longer, shall see a second Abatement; for we shall never stand on even ground in Trade with the Dutch, till Interest be the same with us, as it is with them.

His Majesty was graciously pleased at the opening of the last Session of this Parliament, to propose to the Consideration of both Houses, the Ballancing of the Trade of the Nation; to effect which, in my opinion, the Abatement of Interest is the first and principal Engine which ought to be set on work, which notwithstanding, I should not have presumed to expose it to publick censure, on my own single Opinion, if I had not had the concurrance of much better Judgments then my own; having never seen any thing in Print for it (though much against it) until the latter end of January last; at which time, a Friend whom I had often discoursed with upon this subject, met with by accident a small Tract to the same purpose, Wrote near fifty years ago, which he gave me, and I have, for publick Good, thought fit to annex it hereunto, verbatim.

The Author of the said Tract, by the stile thereof, seems to have been a Country Gentleman, and my Education hath mostly been that of a Merchant, so I hope that going together, they may in some measure, supply the defects of each other.

Another Reason that induced me to to the Printing of them together, is, because what he Wrote then, would be the consequences of the Abatement of Interest from ten to six per cent. I have, I think, fully proved to the Conviction of all Men not wilfully blind, have been the real effects thereof, and that to a greater proportion then he did premise, every Paragraph whereof was Writ by me, and Copies thereof delivered to several worthy Members of this Parliament, many Months before ever I saw or heard of this, or any thing else Writ or Printed to the like purpose.

What I have aimed at in the whole, is the good of my Native Country, otherwise I had not busied my self about it, for I want not employment sufficient of my own, nor have reason to be out of love with that I have.

The several Particulars in the beginning of this Treatise,

relating to Trade, I have only hinted in general terms; hoping that some abler Pen, will hereafter be incited for the service of his King and Country, to enlarge more particularly upon them.

Before I conclude, though I have studied brevity in the whole, I cannot omit the inserting of one Objection more, which I have lately met with, to the main design of this Treatise, viz.

Object. It is said that the lowness of Interest of Money in Holland, is not the EFFECT OF LAWS, but proceeds only FROM THEIR ABUNDANCE THEREOF, for that in Holland, there is no Law limitting the rate of Usury.

Answ. I answer, that it may be true, that in Holland there hath not lately been any Law, to limit Usury to the present rate it is now at, i. e. three or four per cent; although most certain it is, that many years since, there was a Law that did limit it to five or six at most: And by consequence, there would be a renewing of that Law to a lesser rate, were it necessary at this time; It having always been the Policy of that People to keep down the Interest of their Money, three or four per cent, under the rate of what is usually paid in their Neighbouring Countries, which (being now naturally done) it is needless to use the Artificial Stratagem of a Law to Establish.

Answ. 2. Although they have no Law expresly, limitting Interest at present, yet they have other Laws which we cannot yet arrive to, which do effect the same thing among them, and would do the like among us, if we could have them: One whereof, is, their ascertaining REAL SECURITIES by their PUBLICK REGISTERS: For we see evidently, Money is not so much wanting in England as Securities, which Men account Infallible; a remarkable Instance whereof is, the East-India-Company, who can and do take up what Money they please, for four per cent at any time.

Another Law is, Their constitution of BANKS and LUMBARDS, whereby private Persons that have but tollerable credit may be supplied at easie rates from the State.

A third, and very considerable one, is, Their Law for Transferring Bills of Debt, mentioned in the beginning of this Discourse.

A fourth, which is a Custom, and in effect may be here to our Purpose accounted as a Law, is the extraordinary Frugality used in all their Publick Affairs, which in their greatest Extreamities have been such, as not to compel them to give above four per cent for the loan of Money. Whereas it is said, His Majesty in some Cases of exigency, when the National Supplies have not come in to answer the present Emergencies of Affairs, hath been inforced to give above the usual Rates to Gold-Smiths; and that encouraged them to take up great Sums from private Persons at the full rate of six per cent, whereas formerly they usully gave but four per cent otherwise, in humane probability, Money would have fallen of it self to four per cent.

But again, to conclude, Every Nation does proceed according to peculiar Methods of their own in the Transactions of their publick Affairs and Law-making: And in this Kingdom it hath always been the Custom to reduce the Rate of Interest by a Law, when Nature had prepared the matter fit for such an alteration as now I say it hath. By a Law it was reduced from an unlimitted rate, to ten; and afterwards from ten to eight; after that from eight to six. And through the Blessing of Almighty God, this Kingdom hath found, as I think I have fully proved, and every Mans Experience will witness, prodigious success and advantage thereby. And I doubt not, through the like Blessing of God Almighty, but this Generation will find the like great and good effects, by the reduction of it from six to four, which is now at the Birth. And that the next Generation will yet see far greater Advantage by bringing it from four to three per cent.

A DISCOURSE ABOUT TRADE

TRADE AND INTEREST OF MONEY CONSIDERED, &c.

CHAP. I.

A short Reply to a Treatise, entituled, Interest of Money mistaken.

TRADE AND INTEREST OF MONEY CONSIDERED, &c.

CHAP. I.

A short Reply to a Treatise, entituled, Interest of Money mistaken.

There was never any thing propounded for Publick Good, that did not meet with Opposition, arising sometimes from the different apprehensions of men, in regard of the way, who yet have the same design as to the end; sometimes from a dislike of the Person propounding, or the humor of such as would have nothing brought into the World but by their own Midwifery; and are therefore only displeased with a thing, because they were not the first Proposers of it themselves; sometimes from a more inveterate and corrupt Principle of wishing things worse, because they are not well, hating that any thing should be reformed, because they cannot bring all things to the Figure of their own Fancies, and sometimes from other by Respects and private Interests.

Whether any, or which of these hath moved my Opposer, I will not here determine, because I know him not, but leaving that to the Judgment of the impartial Reader, if the Gentleman's love to his Country be such as he professeth, and equal with mine, I shall not doubt but after a more serious Examination of the Matter, he will agree with me in the thing desired.

In the beginning of his Treatise he recites nineteen Obversations of mine, as means whereby the Dutch have encreased their Trade and Riches; And page 9. seems to approve of all them, saying as I told him, as also he doth, page 22. That more might be added, but is not so kind to his Country to let us know what they are; which if he had done, would have been more agreeable to his pretended Candor, and as well of Use to his Country, as an Evidence of his own Sufficiency; it being a much easier thing to cavel at what other men have done, than to present the World with any thing new and material of our own.

Page 10. (passing over many others) he quarrels at that facetious Instance of Noble-Mens wearing in former times Sattin-Doublets, with Canvas backs, which is the most inconsiderable instance of many, yet, upon the whole he concludes with me, That we are much Richer now than we were before any Law for Interest was made, and that we have grown Richer since the abatement of Interest from 10 to 8 per Cent, and yet more Rich since it was abated from 8 to 6 per Cent; which pag. 10. he confesseth, and pag. 11. he implicitly confesseth, and pag. 14. expresly, That according to the more or less Interest any Country pays for Money, the richer or poorer it is. I am glad we are thus far agreed, and that my Opposer is so well instructed, hoping I shall with the less difficulty perswade him to a perfect understanding of the Principle in Controversie, wherein as yet I think it will appear he is no great Master.

But before I enter upon the matter, I must tell the Gentleman, he hath no cause to boast as to that particular Instance concerning Noble Men's former meaner Cloathing; for what I thence inferred was certainly true, as to the time

I spoke of, which was of a time within the memory of a man then living, since Trade was introduced into this Kingdom, which he endeavours to overthrow by an instance out of those times, when Noble men kept multitudes of Retainers about 200 Years past, viz. before Henry the 7th's time, and before Trade was understood in England, which I think is nothing to this purpose. Pag. 11. the Gentleman reciting my Answer to that Objection, That if Interest be abated, the Dutch will call home their Money; to which I replied, that if they should, it would be better for us, The Borrower being always a Slave to the Lender; which he saith, Is no more in the case of English and Dutch, then in that of English and English. And pag. 12. at the beginning, he saith, That I have discovered my design of engrossing all Trade into the Hands of a few rich Merchants, who have Money enough of their own to trade with, to the excluding all young men that want it.

In which two Assertions I appeal to all rational men, whether the Gentleman be not in a very great Error, as to the very nature of the Principle he discourseth? For if one English-man lend to another, be the Interest high or low, between them two nothing is got or lost to the Nation; whereas if a Dutch-man lend Money to an English-man, he at length carries home both Principal and Interest; which Interest, be it more or less, is a clear loss to the Nation, which is so evident, that I hope my Opposer, when he hath thought upon it again, will not upbraid me for begging the Question, because I trouble not the Reader with the particular Proof of those things which I hear no man deny, and therefore conclude every man will grant: For whether Snow be white is not to be disputed.

In his second Assertion likewise, that the abatement of Interest tends to the engrossing of Trade into a few rich mens hands, to the excluding of young men, I appeal to the judgment of all understanding Merchants and rational men, whether the

Gentleman be not miserably mistaken? And whether the never-failing effect of a high Interest all the World over, be not to enrich a few greatly, and impoverish the generality of Traders? So it is in Turkey, where Interest is at 20 per Cent, and upwards, if we may believe those honest and worthy Turkey Merchants, who are now upon the Exchange, and have lived long in that Country; and so it was with us here, when Interest was at 10 per Cent, and upwards, as I have already demonstrated by the instances of Sutton, Gresham, Craven and Spencer; so that he must be naturally blind, or put out his Eyes, who doth not see that the Abatement of Interest is a diffusive Principle: Hence it follows, that as few great and rich Merchants, whose Estates are Personal, (except they have also great Souls) can bear the discourse of abating Interest with more patience than Usurers, well knowing that it must necessarily retrench their present Profits by encreasing the number of Traders; which though it be a small loss to Individuals, will be a vast gain to the generality of the Nation. At the lower end of pag. 12. his Words are, that in my instance of old Audley's observing that 100 l. at 10 per Cent, would in 70 Years amount to 100000 l. he affirms, I am no less mistaken than in other things.

Truly, if I have mistook no more in other things than in that, in such an untrodden Path as this, I have failed much less then I could hope for; to demonstrate which I have here inserted a short Table, shewing that 100 l. at that rate, riseth (within a trifle) to 200 l. in seven Years, Interest upon Interest, so that the usual accompt is and was formerly, that Money doubles once in seven Years, at 10 per Cent, according to which rule 100l. in seventy Years, amounts to 102400 l.

One Hundred Pounds at Ten Pounds per Cent, per Annum, at Interest upon Interest, encreaseth thus, viz.

	L.	S.	D.
At first,	100	00	00
At 3 Months it is	102	10	00
At 6 Months,	105	1	03
At 9 Months,	107	13	9
At 12 Months,	110	07	7
At 1 Year ¼	113	02	9
At 1 Year ½	115	19	4
At 1 Year ¾	118	17	4
At 2 Years	121	16	9
At 2 Years ¼	124	17	8
At 2 Years ½	128	00	1
At 2 Years ¾	131	4	1
At 3 Years	134	9	9
At 3 Years ¼	137	17	0
At 3 Years ½	141	5	10
At 3 Years ¾	144	16	6
At 4 Years	148	8	11
At 4 Years ¼	152	3	1
At 4 Years ½	155	19	2
At 4 Years ¾	159	17	2
At 5 Years	163	17	1
At 5 Years ¼	167	19	0
At 5 Years ½	172	3	0
At 5 Years ¼	176	9	1
At 6 Years	180	17	3
At 6 Years ¼	185	7	9
At 6 Years ½	190	5	0
At 6 Years ¾	194	15	5
At 7 Years	199	12	10

Supposing One Hundred Pounds to double in seven Years at Interest upon Interest, as aforesaid, the encrease is, viz.

	L.
At first	100
At 7 Years	200
At 14 Years	400
At 21 Years	800
At 28 Years	1600
At 35 Years	3200
At 42 Years	6400
At 49 Years	12800
At 56 Years	25600
At 63 Years	51200
At 70 Years	102400

Pag. 13. he saith, That I make use of the abuse of Interest, which no man pleads for, annexing a Discourse against Interest, writ in 1621. when it was at 10 per Cent, endeavouring thereby to impose a Belief that the Gentleman who writ that Discourse was of my mind, whereas it may be supposed the Author of that Book was contented with 8 per Cent, because within four Years after it was brought down to that Rate, and that otherwise he would have writ further, it being probable that he might live till after four Years.

I answer; That through the Mercies of Almighty God, and for the good of this Kingdom, that Patriot of his Country, Old Sr Thomas Culpepper, who I have since been assured was the Author of that Treatise, did live above twenty Years after the writing thereof, and then published a second Treatise, which was lately Re-printed by his worthy Son, which second Treatise is now to be had at Mr Wilkinson's, over against St Dunstan's Church in Fleet-street, which I would advise my Opposer to read, and then I hope he will be more modest hereafter, then to mis-call the most Natural and Rational Conclusions, IMPOSINGS.

But lest he should not meet with the said Treatise, I shall here insert a few Lines out of it to the present purpose, viz.

Old Sr Thomas speaking of the certain good Effects of the Abatement of Interest from 10 to 8 per Cent, pag. 19. of his second Treatise, saith, This good success doth call upon us not to rest here, but that we bring the use for Money to a lower rate, which now I suppose will find no Opposition, for all Objections which before the Statute were made against it, are now answered by the Success, & most certainly the benefit will be much greater to the Common wealth, by calling the Use for Money down from 8 to 5 or 6 per Cent, then it was from calling it down from 10 to 8 per Cent. I shall not Comment upon his Words, but only declare that in truth, I never heard of this Treatise, nor of any other to the like effect, when I write mine.

Pag. 13. the Gentle-man brings up his Battalia, and like a stout Champion for the slie and timerous heard-of Usurers, plants his main Battery against that part which I confessed to be weakest, viz. that the difficulty of this Question is, Whether the lowness of Interest be the cause or the Effect of Riches? And he positively denies that the lowness of Interest is the Cause, & affirms it to be only the Effect thereof, which he endeavours to prove by four Arguments, which I shall particularly answer in a due place, in the mean time use my own Method to prove, That the Abatement of Interest by a Law in England will be a means to improve the Riches of this Kingdom: And I prove it thus;

1.	Whatever doth	Advance the value of Land in Purchase,	must be a procuring cause of Riches
2.		Improve the Rent of Farms,	
3.		Encrease the bulk of Foreign Trade,	
4.		Multiply domestick Artificers,	
5.		Encline the Nation to Thriftiness,	
6.		Employ the Poor,	
7.		Encrease the Stock of People,	

Now that the abatement of Interest, will advance the value of Land, I prove first by Experience, for certainly Anno 1621. the currant price of our Lands in England was twelve Years purchase; and so I have been assured by many antient Men whom I have queried particularly as to this Matter; and I find it so by purchases made about that time by my own Relations and Acquaintance, and I presume that any Nobleman or Gentleman of England, by only commanding the Stewards of their Mannors to give them Lists out of the Records of any Mannors or Farms that their Grand-Fathers, or Fathers bought or sold fifty Years past, will find that the same Farms to be now sold, would yield (one with another) at least treble the Mony, and in some cases six times the Mony they were then bought and sold for; which I submit still to the single and joynt Judgments of the honourable Members of both Houses of Parliament, who being the greatest Owners of our Territory, are in their private, as well as in their politick Capacities, the most proper and experimental Judges of this Case; if the Antient of them will please to recollect their Memories, and the Younger will please to be informed by their Elder Servants; and if this be so, it cannot be denied, but the abatement of Interest by a Law, hath greatly advanced Lands in purchase as well as improved Rents, by meliorating the Lands themselves, those improvements by marling, limeing, draining, &c. having been made since Money was at 8 and 6 per cent, which 10 per cent could not bear.

And to prove that Lands were then at twelve Years purchase, I have the written Testimony of that incomparable worthy Person Sr Thomas Culpepper Senior, who, page 11. of his first Treatise, expresly affirms, That Land was then at twelve Years Purchase; who being himself a grave and antient Parliament Man, and dedicating his Book to the then Parliament, whereof he was then a Member, cannot without horrible uncharitableness, be presumed to impose upon his Country.

And now that our Interest is at 6 per cent, as the same worthy Author did wisely fore-see, I appeal to the Judgment and Experience of my Country Men, whether the genuine price of our Lands in England now would not be 20 Years Purchase, were it not for accidental Pressures, under which it labours at present, such as these;

1. Our late great Land Taxes.

2. And principally the late great Improvement of Ireland, mentioned in my former Treatise, the consequence whereof is, that that Country now supplieth Foreign Markets, as well as our own Plantations in America, with Beef, Pork, Hides, Tallow, Bread, Beer, Wool and Corn, at cheaper Rates then we can afford, to the beating us out of those Trades, whereas formerly, viz. presently after the late Irish War, many Men got good Estates by Transporting English Cattle thither.

And that the Improvement of Ireland, is the principal cause why our Lands in purchase rise not as naturally they should, with the fall of our Interest, appears evidently from the effect the fall of Interest hath had upon Houses in London; where the growth of Ireland could have no such destructive influence, which hath been so considerable, that whosoever will please to inform themselves by old Scriveners, or antient Deeds, shall find, that a House in London, about fifty Years past, that would sell but for 300l. at most, would readily sell within a short time after Interest was brought to 8 per cent, at 5 or 600 l. and the same Houses to be sold sometime after Interest was brought to 6 per cent, viz. before and after the late Dutch War, would have yielded without scruple 1000 or 1200l. The abatement of Interest having had a double effect upon Houses, by encreasing Trade, and consequently raising Rents, as well as encreasing the number of Years purchase.

3. A third reason why Land doth not at present bear an exact proportion to 6 per cent, which should naturally be

twenty Years, is the late Plague, which did much depopulate this Kingdom.

4. The late Fire in London, which hath engaged Men in Building in the City, who otherwise would have been purchasing in the Country.

5. The unusal plenty of Corn, which hath been for these three or four Years past in most parts of Christendom, the like whereof hath been seldom known, it happening most commonly that when one Country hath had great plenty, others have had great scarcity.

6. The racking up of Rents in the Years 1651. and 1652. which was presently after the last abatement of Interest.

A seventh accidental Reason why Land doth not sell at present, at the rate it naturally should, in proportion to the legal Interest, is, that innovated practice of Bankers in London, which hath more effects attending it then most I converse with have yet observed; but I shall here take notice of that only which is to my present purpose, viz.

The Gentlemen that are Bankers, having a large Interest from his Majesty, for what they advance upon his Majesties Revenue; can afford to give the full legal Interest to all Persons that put Money into their hands, though for never so short or long a time, which makes the trade of Usury so easie, and hitherto safe, that few, after having found the sweetness of this lasie way of emprovement (being by continuance and success grown to fancy themselves secure in it) can be lead (there being neither ease nor profit to invite them) to lay out their Money in Land, though at 15 Years purchase; whereas before this way of private Bankering came up, men that had Money were forced ofttimes to let it lie dead by them, until they could meet with Securities to their minds; and if the like necessity were now of Money lying dead, the loss of use for the dead time being deducted from the profit of 6 l. per Cent, (communibus annis) would in effect take off 1 l. per Cent per Annum of the profit of Usury, and consequently incline men more to purchase Lands, in regard the difference between Usury and Purchasing would not in point of profit be so great as now it is; this new invention of Cashciring, having in my opinion clearly bettered the Usurers trade 1 or 2 per Cent per Annum. And that this way of leaving Money with Gold-Smiths hath had the aforesaid effect, seems evident to me from the scarcity it makes of Money in the Country; for the Trade of Bankers being only in London, doth very much drain the ready Money from all other parts of the Kingdom.

The second point I am to prove, is, That it will advance the Rent of Farms.

To prove that it did so in fact, depends on memory; and for my own part, I and most others I converse with, do perfectly remember that Rents did generally rise after the late abatement of Interest, (viz.) in the year 1651. and 1652.

The reason why they did so, was from the encouragement which that abatement of Interest gave to Landlords and Tenants, to improve by Draining, Marling, Limeing, &c. excellently made out by the aforesaid two worthy Authors, so that I do (I think with good Reason) conclude that the present fall of Rents is not natural, but accidental, and to be ascribed principally to the fore-going Reasons, given for the present abatement of Land in purchase, and especially to the late Improvement of Ireland.

The third thing I am to prove, is, That the abatement of Interest will encrease the bulk of foreign Trade, which I do thus.

By evidence of fact, it hath been so in England, the encrease of our Trade hath always followed the abatement of our Interest by Law, I say, not preceded, but followed it, and the Cause doth always go before the Effect, which I think I have evidently demonstrated in my former Treatise.

If any doubt of this, and will be at the pains to examin the Customhouse Books, they may soon be resolved.

2. By Authority; not only of that antient Gentleman Sr Thomas Culpepper in his second Treatise, and therein of the judgment of the French King and Court, in an Edict there recited, but likewise of a Parliament of England, King, Lords & Commons, in the Act for reducing it to 6 per Cent, in the Preamble whereof are these Words, viz. Forasmuch as the Abatement of Interest from 10 in the Hundred in former times, hath been found by notable Experience beneficial to the Advancement of Trade, and Improvement of Lands by good Husbandry, with many other considerable Advantages to this Nation, especially the reducing of it to a nearer proportion with foreign States, with whom we traffick: And whereas in fresh memory the like fall from 8 to 6 in the Hundred by a late constant Practice hath found the like success to the general contentment of this Nation, as is visible by several Improvements, &c.

3. By necessary consequence; when Interest is abated, they who call in their Money must either buy Land, or trade with it: If they buy Land the many Buyers will raise the price of Land: If they trade they encrease the number of Traders, and consequently the bulk of Trade; and let their Money lie dead by them, I think I have fully proved they cannot; in an addition I published to my first Observations.

4. By reason; for first whilst Interest is at 6 per Cent, no man will run an adventure to Sea for the gain of 8 or 9 per Cent, which the Dutch having Money at 4 or 3 per Cent at Interest are contented with, and therefore can and do follow a vast trade in Salt from St Vuall, Rochel, and other parts to the Baltique Seas, and also their fishing Trade for Herrings and Whale-fishing, which we neglect, as being not worth our trouble and hazard, while we can make 6 per Cent of our Money sleeping.

For the measure of Money employed in Trade in any Nation bears an exact proportion to the Interest paid for Money; As for instance, when Money was at 10 per Cent in England, no man in his wits would follow any Trade whereby he did not promise himself 14 or 12 per Cent gain at least, when Interest was at 8, the hopes of 12 or 10 at least was necessary, as 8 or 9 per Cent is, now Interest goes at 6 per Cent, the Infallible Consequence whereof is, that the Trades before recited, as well as those of Muscovy and Greenland, and so much at least of all others, that will not afford us a clear profit of 8 or 9 per Cent, we carelesly give away to the Dutch, and must do so forever, unless we bring our Interest nearer to a Par with theirs; and hence in my poor Opinion it follows very clearly, that if our Interest were abated one third part, it would occasion the employment of one third part more of Men, Shiping and Stock, in foreign and domestick Trades.

This discovers the vanity of all our Attempts for gaining of the White-Herring Fishing-Trade, of which the Dutch, as every body observes, make wonderful great advantage, though the Fish be taken upon our own Coasts; I wish as many did take notice of the reason of it, which therefore I shall say something of now, though I have touched it in my former Treatise.

The plain case is this, A Dutch-man will be content to employ a Stock of 5 or 10000 l. in Burses, materials for Fishing, Victuals, &c. for the carrying on of this Trade, and if at the winding up of his Accounts, he finds he hath got clear, communibus annis, for his Stock and Adventure 5 per Cent per Annum, he thanks God, and tells his Neighbours he hath had a thriving Trade: Now while every sloathful ignorant man with us, that hath but wit enough to tell out his Money to a Gold Smith, can get 6 per Cent without pains or care; Is it not monstrous absurd to imagine that ever the English will do any good upon this Trade, till they begin at the right end, which must be to reduce the Interest of Money?

Secondly, The depraved nature of man affecting ease and pleasure, while use of Money runs at 6 per Cent, hath always at hand an easie expedient to indulge that humor, and reconcile it to another as considerable, viz. his Covetousness, by putting his Money to use; and if a Merchant through his youthful care and industry, arrive to an Estate of 20000 l. in twenty Years trading, whilst Money is so high, and Land so low, he can easily turn Country Gentleman or Usurer, which were Interest of Money at 4 per Cent he could not do; and consequently must not only follow his Trade himself, but make his Children Traders also; for to leave them Money without skill to use it, would advantage little, and purchasing of Lands less, when the fall of Interest shall raise them to twenty or thirty Years purchase, which I hope yet to live to see.

Thirdly, From this necessity of Merchants keeping to their Trade, and Childrens succeeding their Fathers therein, would ensue to Merchants greater skill in Trade, more exact and certain correspondency, surer & more trusty Factors abroad, & those better acquainted & concatinated together by the experimental links of each others Humors, Stile, Estate and Business. And whereas it is as much as a prudent man can do in ten Years time, after his settling in London, to be exactly well fitted with Factors in all parts, and those by Correspondency brought into a mutual Acquaintance of each other, and honest Work-men and Masters of Ships, &c. And by that time he hath traded ten Years longer, if he succeed well, it is six to one but he leaves Trade, and turns Country Gentleman, or Usurer, and so that profitable Engine, (the Wheels whereof by Correspondency move one another in many parts of the World) which he hath been so long a framing, within a few Years after it is brought to work well, is broken to pieces, and the benefit thereof to the Kingdom (which is ten times more then to him that made it) is lost, whereas in Holland and Italy, where Money is at 3 and 4 per Cent, and consequently Merchants forc'd to keep and trust to their Trades only, their Businesses are, and must be so ordered and carried on from the beginning, that when a Man dies, the Trade is no more disturbed then when the Wife dies in England.

I am ashamed of the odious Prolixity and Repetition I am (contrary to my Nature) forced to use; but my Opposer doth so often, and I think disingenuously upbraid me with begging the Question, that I am compelled to it.

The fourth thing I am to prove, is, that It multiplies Domestick Artificers.

If the former be true, that it encreases foreign Trade, I suppose no man will have the confidence to deny this to be a necessary and infallible consequence of that: For we see throughout the World, where-ever there is the greatest Trade, there are the most Artificers, and that since our own Trade encreased in England, our Artificers of all sorts are proportionably encreased. The building of London hath made multitudes of Bricklayers and Carpenters; much use of Shiping will make Ships dear, and the dearness of Shiping will make many Shipwrights; much foreign Trade will encrease the vent of our Native Manufactures, and much vent will make many work-men; and if we cannot get and breed them fast enough our selves, we shall draw them from foreign parts, as the Dutch draw away ours, it being a wise and true observation of (as I remember) Sr Walter Rawleigh, That no Nation can want People that hath good Laws.

The fifth thing to be proved, is, that It enclines a Nation to thriftiness; this is likewise consequent to the former, and by experience made good in England; for since our Trade encreased, though the generality of our Nation are grown richer, as I have shewed, and consequently more splendid in Clothes, Plate, Jewels, Houshold-stuff, and all other outward signs of

Riches; yet are we not half so much given to Hospitality and good House-keeping (as it is called) as in former dayes, when our greatest Expence was upon our Bellies, the most destructive Consumption that can happen to a Nation, and tending only to nourish Idleness, Luxury and Beggary; whereas that other kind of Expence which follows Trade, encourageth Labour, Arts and Invention: To which give me leave to add, that The abatement of Interest conjoynt with Excises upon our home consumption (if the later could be hit upon without disturbance to Trade, or danger of continuation) are two of the most comprehensive and effectual Sumptuary Laws that ever were established in any Nation, and most necessitating and engaging any People to thriftiness, the high Road to Riches, as well for Nations as private Families.

The frugal Italians of Old, and the provident Dutch of latter times I think have given the World a sufficient proof of this Theorim; and if any shall tell me, it is the nature of those People to be thrifty; I answer, all men by nature are alike; it is only Laws, Custom, and Education that differ men; their Nature and Disposition, and the disposition of all People in the World proceed from their Laws; the French Peasantry are a slavish, cowardly People, because the Laws of their Country have made them Slaves; the French Gentry, a noble, valiant People, because free by Law, Birth and Education: In England we are all free Subjects by our Laws, and therefore our People prove generally couragious; the Dutch and Italians are both frugal Nations, though their Climates and Governments differ as much as any, because the Laws of both Nations encline them to Thriftiness; other Nations I could name, are generally vain & prodigal, not by Nature, nor for want of a good Country; but because their Laws, &c. dispose them so to be.

The sixth proof of the Proposition, is, that It employes the Poor; which is a necessary Consequence likewise of the encrease of Trade in Cities, and Emprovement of Land in the Country, which is well and truly demonstrated from Experience, by the Elder and Younger Sr Thomas Culpepper, to whom to avoid Prolixity, I must refer the Reader.

Seventhly, It encreaseth the People of a Nation; this also necessarily followeth the encrease of Trade and Emprovement of Lands, not that it causeth married men to get more Children.

But 1st, a trading Country affording comfortable Subsistances to more Families then a Country destitute of Trade, is the reason that many do marry, who otherwise must be forc'd to live single, which may be one reason why fewer People of either Sex are to be seen unmarried in Holland at 25 years of age, then may be found in England at 40 years old.

2dly, Where there is much Employment, and good Pay, if we want Hands of our own, we shall draw them from others, as hath been said.

3dly, We shall keep our own People at home, which otherwise for want of Employment would be forcd to leave us, and serve other Nations, as too many of our Sea-men, Ship-wrights, and others have done.

4thly, Our Lands and Trade being improved, will render us capable not only of employing, but feeding a far greater number of People, as is manifest in that instance of the Land of Palestine.

And if these will be the effects of abating Interest, then I think it is out of doubt that the Abatement of Interest is the cause of the encrease of the Riches of any Kingdom, for quicquid efficit tale est magis tale. Now to answer his four recited Reasons, viz.

First, he saith, If a low stated Interest by Law be the cause of Riches, no Country would be poor, all desiring Riches rather then Poverty, and all having it in their power to state their Interest as low as they please by Law.

I answer, first, Whatever Nation doth it gradually, for so it must be done; as it hath been hitherto in England (2 per Cent being enough to abate at one time) will find those effects I have mentioned; but it is a work of Ages, and cannot be done at once; For Nec natura aut lex operantur per saltum.

Secondly, It is great Imprudence to imagine that any Country understanding their true Interest so well, as by degrees to abate Use-Money, will not likewise by the same Wisdom be led to the instituting of many other good Laws for the encouragement of Trade, as our Parliaments have still proceeded to do, as Interest hath been abated.

His second Reason is, That if the lowness of Interest were not the effect of Riches in Holland, they might take as much Use-Money as they could get, there being no Law against it.

I answer, There were formerly Laws in Holland that reduced Interest to 8 and 6, and afterwards to 5 per Cent, Anno 1640. and since in the Year 1655. to 4 per Cent, the Placart for which I have seen, and have been told, and do believe they have since reduced it by Placart to 3 per Cent, as to their Cantors, and all publick Receipts, which in Holland is as much in effect as if they had made a general Law for it, because the most of their Receipts and Payments are made in and out of the aforesaid publick Offices, or else into and out of their Banks, for which no Use-Money is allowed; which several gradual and succesful Abatements of Interest did occasion their Riches at first, and brought their People to that consistency of Wealth, that they have since wrought themselves into such an abundance, that there are more Lenders now than Borrowers, and so I doubt not but it will be with us in a few Years, after the next Abatement of Interest is made by Law; which I have good reason to conclude, not only from the visible operations of nature in all other things and places, but from Fact and Experience in this very case; being certain that the Gold-Smiths in London could have what

Money they would upon their Servants Notes only, at 4 l. and 4 l. 10 s. per Cent, before the late Emergencies of State, which I could demonstrate, have very much obstructed the natural fall of Interest with us; something more I have said in answer to this in the addition to my former Treatise; and this may serve likewise for an answer to his third Reason.

Fourthly, he saith, That which I must prove to make good my Assertion, is, that any Country in the World from a poor and low condition, while Interest was at 6 per Cent, was made rich by bringing it to 4 per Cent, or 3 per Cent by a Law.

I answer, If the instance of Holland and Italy were not sufficient to satisfie him in this point, yet that having proved (which he cannot deny) that our own Kingdom hath been enriched consequently, constantly and proportionably to and after our several Abatements of Interest by Law, from an unlimitted rate, to 10, from 10 to 8, and from 8 to 6 per Cent, I think it may rationally be concluded that another Abatement of Interest in England would cause a further encrease of Riches, as it hath done in Holland.

From Italy I have endeavoured to gain a certain accompt of their legal Interest, but am advised that no taking of Use-Money is allowed by their Pontificial Laws, the Interest now taken there, which is generally 4 per Cent, is done only by dispensation of Pope Paul the fifth, and that notwithstanding no man can recover Interest of Money there, if the party who should pay it can prove he hath no gained the value of the Interest demanded: Now let the Reader judge whether that practise of Holland, and this of Italy, where the Romish Churchmen have so great power, who are to take Cognizance, and may by their Auricular Confessors, of all Offences of this kind; the Laws concerning the use of Money in those Countries being Pontificial, do not amount in effect to a low stated Interest by Law in England.

But to deal more ingenuously with my Opposer then he hath done with me, I will grant him that much Riches will occasion in any Kingdom a low rate of Interest, and yet that doth not hinder but a low stated Interest by Law may be a cause of Riches: For if Trade be that which enricheth any Kingdom, and lowering of Interest advanceth Trade (which I think is sufficiently proved) then the Abatement of Interest, or more properly restraining of Usury; which the antient Romans, and all other wise and rich People in the world did always drive at, is doubtless a primary and principal cause of the Riches of any Nation; it being not improper to say, nor absurd to conceive, that The same thing may be both a Cause and an Effect. Peace begets Plenty, and Plenty may be a means to preserve Peace: Fear begets Hatred, and Hatred Fear: The diligent Hand makes rich, and Riches makes men diligent, so true is the Proverb, Crescit amor Nummi, quantum ipsa pecunia erescit; Love we say begets Love, the fertility of a Country may cause the encrease of People, and the encrease of People may cause the further and greater fertility of a Country; Liberty and Property conduce to the encrease of Trade and Emprovement of any Country; and the encrease of Trade and Emprovements conduce to the procuring, as well as securing of Liberty and Property; Strength and Health conduce to a good digestion, and a good digestion is necessary to the preservation of Health and encrease of Strength; and as a Person of very great honour pertinently instanced at a late debate upon this Question, An Egg is the cause of a Hen, and a Hen the cause of an Egg. The incomparable Lord Bacon in his History of Henry the 7th, saith, pag. 245, of that Prince as well as other men, That his Fortune worked upon his Nature, & his Nature upon his Fortune; the like may be said of Nations; The Abatement of Interest causeth an encrease of Wealth, and the encrease of Wealth may cause a further Abatement of Interest. But that is best done by the Midwifery of good Laws, which is what I plead for; the corrupt Nature of man being more apt to decline to Vice, then incline to Vertue.

Folio 15. he affirms, Lands are not risen in Purchase, nor Rents improved since the Abatement of Interest.

That I shall say no more to, it is matter of Fact, and Gentlemen who are the Owners of Land are the best Judges of this case, only I would entreat them not to depend upon their Memories alone, but to command particular accompts to be given them what sum or sums of Money were given 40 or 50 Years past for any intire Farms or Mannors they now know; and I doubt not but they will find that most of them will yield double the said sums of Money now, notwithstanding the present great pressures that Land lies under, which ought maturely to be considered of, when this judgment is made, I rather desire the enquiry to be made upon the gross sum of Money paid, then the Years purchase, as being less fallible, because many Farms have been of late Years so rackt up in Rents, that it may be they will not yield more Years purchase now, according to the present Rents, then they would many years past, and yet may yield double the Money they were then bought or sold for, because the Rents were much less then.

Fol. 15. he impertinently quarrels at my instance of Ireland, saying, I quote it sometimes to prove the benefit of a low Interest, pag. 8. And sometimes the mischief of high Interest, pag. 9. Which seems to me to be an unfriendly way of prevaricating: For pag. 8. I mention the late great improvement of Ireland only, as an accidental cause why our Rents at that present fell, and in this it appears I was not much mistaken, for within a few Moneths after I first writ that Treatise, the Parliament took notice of it. Pag. 9. I mention that place among others, that pay a high Interest, and are consequently very poor; if there be any contradiction in this, let the Reader judge. Pag. 16.

the Gentleman puzleth himself about finding Mistakes in my Calculation of the encrease of Merchants Estates, but discovers none but his own; so I shall not trouble the Reader further about that, all Merchants granting me as much as I design by it, though some of them have not, or care not to observe the Abatement of Interest to have been the principal cause thereof.

Fol. 17. Because he cannot answer that large and pregnant instance of the effects of a low Interest which I gave, in the case of the Sugar-Bakers of London ,and those of Holland, which was but one of a hundred, which I could have mentioned; he endeavours to set up another of a contrary effect, which is a weak rediculous Instance, and nothing to his purpose; for that Commodity that I mentioned, viz. Sugar, is a solid bulky Commodity, always in fashion, not consequent to humor, as is that of Silk-Stockings, 1000l. worth whereof may be with less charge carried to Italy, then 30l. worth of Barbadoes Sugar can be sent to Holland: Besides, the reason why we of late sent Silk-Stockings thither, is accidental, not natural, only happening by means of an Engin we have to weave them, whereof they have not yet the use in Italy: Besides, wearing things being more esteemed through Fancy then Judgment, the Italians may have the same Vanity, which is too much amongst us, to esteem that which is none of their own making, as we do French Ribonds, and the French-men English ones; besides, he is mistaken in saying we bring the Silk we make them of from Italy, for the Silk of which we make that Commodity is Turky, not Italian Silk.

Fol. 18. The Gentleman begins to be kind, and finding me out of the way, pretends to set me right, viz. to instruct me, as first, what will bring down Interest.

1st, Multitude of People.

2dly, A full Trade.

3dly, Liberty of Conscience.

I Answer; That I have I think proved, that the Abatement of Interest will effect the two former, and I think my Opposer is not clear sighted, if he cannot discern that the latter, in a due and regulated proportion must be a consequent of them.

In the next place, the Gentleman finding me at a loss, as he says, for the reason of our great Trade at present, will help me as well as he can.

I answer; Those latter Words (as well as he can) were well put in, for as yet he hath told me no News, nor given any shadow of Reason, that I knew not before, and had maturely considered on many Years before I writ the first Treatise.

The Reasons he gives for our present greatness of Trade are;

First, Our casting off the Church of Rome.

Secondly, The Statutes in Henry the 7th's time, prohibiting Noble mens Retainers, and making their Lands liable to the payment of Debts.

Thirdly, The discovery of the East and West-India Trades, pag. 19, 20.

To his first and second Reasons, I answer, that Those Statutes of Henry the 7th, and our casting off the Church of Rome, did long precede our being any thing in Trade; which began not until the latter end of Queen Elizabeth's Reign, and afterwards encreased in the time of King James and King Charles the first, as we abated our Interest, and not otherwise; there being a Person yet living, and but 77 Years of Age, viz. Captain Russel of Wapping, who assures me he can remember since we had not above three Merchants Ships of 300 Tuns, and upwards, belonging to England.

Secondly, That in Italy where there are no such Statutes for abridgement of Noble men's Retainers, nor casting off the Church of Rome, there is notwithstanding a very great Trade, and Land at from 35 to 40 Years purchase, which sufficiently shews that a low Interest is absolutely and principally necessary, and that the other particulars alone will not do, to the procuring of those ends, although a low Interest singly doth it in Italy.

To his third Reason, I answer, that There are some men yet living who do remember a greater Trade to East-India, and a far greater Stock employed therein, then we have now; and yet we were so far from thriving upon it, that we lost by it, and could never see our principal Money again; Nor ever did we greatly prosper upon it, till our Interest was much abated by Laws; nor ever shall mate the Dutch in it, till our Interest be as low as theirs. The like, in a great measure, is true in our West-India Trades, we never got considerable by them till our last Abatement of Interest from 8 to 6 per Cent.

Pag. 21, 22. he labours to prove, that If we would have Trade to flourish, and Lands high, we must imitate the Hollanders in their Practices; which in matter of Trade I know is most certain, so far as they are consistent with the Government of our own Country: And the first and readiest thing wherein we can imitate them, is to reduce our Interest of Money to a lower rate, after the manner of our Fathers, and they did it before us, which will naturally lead us to all the other advantages in Trade which they now use.

1. For, If Interest be abated to 4 per Cent who will not, that can leave his Children any competent Estate of 1000 or 2000 l. each, bring them up to Writing, Arithmetick, and Merchants Accompts, and instruct them in Trades, well knowing that the bare use of their Money, or the product of it in Land will scarce keep them.

2. Must not all Persons live lower in Expence, when all Trades will be less gainful to Individuals, though more profitable to the Publick?

3. Will it not put us upon building as bulky and cheap sailing Ships as they?

4. Will it not bring Trade to be so familiar amongst us, that

our Gentlemen, who are in our greatest Councils, will come to understand it, and accordingly contrive Laws in favour of it?

5. Will not; nay, hath it not already brought us to lower our Customs upon our own native Commodities and Manufactures?

6. Will it not in time bring us to transferring Bills of Debt? Is not necessity the Mother of Invention, and that old Proverb true, facile est inventis addere? There is in my poor Opinion nothing conduceable to the good of Trade, that we shall not by one accident or other hit upon, when we have attained this Fundamental point, and are thereby necessitated to follow and keep to our Trades from Generation to Generation.

7. Do we not see that even as the World now goes, dies diem docet, scarce a Session of Parliament passeth without making some good Acts for the bettering of Trade, and pareing off the extravagancy of the Law; for which ends this last Session produced three.

That about the Silk-Throwsters.

That about Transportation of Hides, &c.

That about Writs of Error.

8. Will not the full understanding of Trade (acquired by Experience, and never wanting to any People that make it their constant business to follow Trade, as we must do when Interest shall be at 4 per Cent) quickly bring us to find our advantage in permitting all Strangers to co-habit, trade and purchase Lands amongst us upon as easie terms as the Dutch do?

Will not the Consequence of this Law, by augmenting the value of Land, bring us in time to regular and just Enclosements of our Forrests, Commons and Wastes, and making our smaller Rivers navigable? the highest Improvements that this Land is capable of: And have not these last 50 Years, since the several Abatements of Interest, produced more of these profitable Works then 200 Years before?

Will not the Consequence of this Law discover to us the

vanity and opposition to Trade that there seems to be in many of our Statutes yet in force, such as these following, viz.

1st, The Statutes of Bankrupt (as they are now used) in many cases more to the Prejudice of honest Dealers then the Bankrupt himself, by compelling men often times to refund Money received of the Bankrupt for Wares justly sold and delivered him, long before it was possible for the Seller to discover the Buyer to be a Brankrupt.

2dly, Such are our Laws limiting the price of Beer and Ale to one Penny per Quart, which bar us from all Improvements and Imitation of foreign Liquors made of Corn, commonly called Mum, Spruce-Beer, Rosteker-Beer, which may, and are made in England, and would occasion the profitable Consumption of an incredible quantity of our Grain, and prove a great addition to his Majesties Revenue of Excise, expend abundance of Coals in long boyling of those Commodities, imploy many Hands in the Manufacture of them, as well as Shipping in Transportation of them, not only to all our own Plantations in America, but to many other parts of the World.

3dly, Our Laws against engrossing Corn and other Commodities, there being no Persons more beneficial to Trade in a Nation, then Engrossers, which will be a worthy Employment for our present Usurers, and render them truly useful to their Country.

4thly, Such was our Law against Exportation of Bullion lately repealed.

5thly, Such is the use of the Law at present, which takes not only a Custom, but 15 s. per Tun Excise on strong Beer exported, being the same Rate it pays when spent at home, contrary to the practice of all trading Countries.

6thly, Such are our Laws which charge Sea-Coals, or any of our native Provisions exported with Custom, viz. Beef, Pork, Bread, Beer, &c. for which I think in prudence the Door should be opened wide to let them out.

7thly, Of the like nature is our Law imposing a great duty upon our Horses, Mares and Nags exported.

8. Such in my weak Opinion, is that branch of the Statute of 5 Eliz. that none should use any manual Occupation, except he hath been Appretince to the same.

9thly, Such (in my Opinion) is the Law which yet prohibits the Exportation of our own Coin; for since it is now by consent of Parliament agreed and found by experience of all understanding men, to be advantagious for this Kingdom to permit the free Exportation of Bullion, I think it were better for us that our own Coin might likewise be freely exported, because by what of that went out, we should gain the Manufacture (the Coyning) besides the great honour and note of Magnificency it would be to his Majesty and this Kingdom, to have his Majesty's Coin currant in all parts of the Universe.

10thly, Such are all by-Laws used among the Society of Coopers, & other Artificers, limiting Masters to keep but one Apprentice at a time; whereas it were better for the publick, they were permitted to keep ten, if they could or would maintain or employ them.

11thly, Such seem to be many of our Laws relating to the Poor, especially those against Inmates in Cities & trading Towns, and those obliging Parishes to maintain their own Poor only.

Page 23. and 24. the Gentleman makes a large Repetition of what he had said before, wherein I observe, nothing new but that he saith, the East-India-Company have Money at 4. per cent, only because Men may have their Money out when they please, which is a mistake, though a small one, for the Company seldom or never take up Money but for a certain time, though I doubt not but that Generous Company will, and do at most times, accommodate any Person with his Money before due, that hath occasion to require such a kindness of them, although they oblige not themselves to do it.

In this tenth particular, at the latter end of page 24. he saith, I am mistaken in my Assertion of the Interest of Scotland, which upon further enquiry amongst the Scotch Merchants upon the Exchange, I am told is his own mistake; So I must leave that, being matter of fact, to those that know that Country and its Laws, more and better then either of us: Lastly, he concludes, that whilst I say the matter in England is so naturally prepared for an Abatement of Interest, that it cannot be long obstructed: I propound a Law to anticipate Nature, which is against Reason.

I answer, it was the Wisdom of our Grand-fathers to bring it to what it would bear in their time; and our Fathers found the good effects of that, and brought it lower, and the benefit thereof is since manifested to us by the success; and therefore, seeing the matter will now bear further Abatement; it is reasonable for us to follow that excellent Example of our Ancestors; Laws against Nature I grant would be ineffectual; but I never heard before, that Laws to help Nature, were against Reason.

Touching the Gentleman's personal Reflections upon me, I shall say little, it appears sufficiently by what I have writ, and his Answer, that I am an Advocate for Industry, he for Idleness: It appears likewise to those that know me in London, which are many, that I am so far from designing to engrose Trade, that I am hastening to convert what I can of my small Estate that is personal, into real, supposing it to be my Interest so to do, before the Use of Money falls, which I conclude cannot long suspend, and that then Land and Houses must rise; and I doubt it will appear, when this Gentleman is as well known as I am, that he is more an Usurer, then an Owner of Land or Manager of Trade at present; my ends have only been to serve my Country, which I can with a sincere Heart declare, in the Presence of God and Men: And that nothing else could have engaged me into this unpleasing Controversie, wherein I have given unwilling offence to all my nearest Relations, and knew at first that I must needs do so, most of them being such as Age and Wisdom hath instructed rather to be Box-keepers then Gamesters.

I have before-mentioned the Judgment of the French King and Court, but intended not to recite the Edict, being it is at large in Sr Thomas Culpepper ssenior his last Treatise, yet on second thoughts, considering all Men perhaps, may not come to a sight of that, and finding the said Edict so comprehensive of the whole matter of this Controversie, I have here recited it.

The King by these Edicts had nothing relieved the necessities of the Nobility, if he had not provided for Usuries, which have ruined many good and antient Houses; filled Towns with unprofitable Servants, and the Countries with Miseries and Inhumanities; he found the Rents viz. Usuries constituted after 10 or 8 in the hundred, did ruin many good Families, hindred the Traffick and Commerce of Merchandize's, and made Tillage and Handicrafts to be neglected, many desiring through the easiness of a deceitful Gain to live Idlely in good Towns of their Rents, rather then to give themselves with any pains to liberal Arts, or to till or husband their Inheritances: For this reason, meaning to invite his subjects to enrich themselves with more just Gain, to content themselves with more moderate profit, and to give the Nobility means to pay their Debts; he did forbid all Usury or Constitution of Rents at an higher rate then six Pounds five Shillings in the hundred.

The Edict was verified in the Court of Parliament, which considered that it was always prejudicial to the Commonwealth, to give Money to Usury; for it is a Serpent whose biteing is not apparent, and yet it is so sensible, that it peirceth the very Hearts of the best Families.

The whole of this Controversie lies narrowly in these two

short Questions, viz. Will abatement of Interest improve Trade? Secondly, Will it advance the price of Land? The collective united Bodies of the Government of our own and other Kingdoms, expresly say it will do both, and Experience cries aloud that so it will do, and hath done in all Ages and in all Places; and I never yet met with any private person, how much soever concerned in Interest, that had the ignorance or confidence to deny both.

For discourse with a Country Usurer, he will affirm, and perhaps be ready to swear to it, that this abatement of Interest is a Knavish design of the Citizens to advance themselves, who are too proud already; and that if it go forward it will undo all the Country Gentlemen in England: And if one speak with the City Usurers, they will be as ready to affirm, that this is a plot carried on only by Noblemen and Gentlemen, whose Estates are all in Land, for their own advantage, and that it will spoil all the Trade of the Kingdom, being a project at one instant to take off just one third of all Mens Estates that are personal, and add the same proportion to all such whose Estates are real; which in effect is to Impoverish all the Younger, and Enrich all Elder Brothers in England: So that out of the Mouthes of the greatest and wisest Adversaries to this principle, it may be justly concluded, that though singlely they deny the truth of it, yet joyntly they confess it.

To conclude, there is nothing that I have said, or that I think any other can say upon this occasion, but was said in substance before by old Sr Thomas Culpepper (though unknown to me) who had an ampel and clear sight into the whole nature of this Principle, and the true effects and consequences of it, Truth being always the same, though Illustrations may vary; nor can any thing now be objected against the making a Law for a further abatement of Interest, but the same that was objected in those times wherein the former Statutes past; so that why my

Opposer should cavil at the doing of that by a Law in England, now (which he seems to like well, if it could be done) I know no real cause, except it be that in truth he is wise enough to know that a Law in England will certainly do the Work, as it hath done formerly, and in consequence his own private Gain will be retrenched.

Before I concluded I think it necessary, for caution to my Country-men, to let them know what effects these discourses have had on others; when I wrote my first Treatise, Interest was in the Island of Barbadoes at 15 per centum, where it is since by an Act of the Country brought down to 10 per cent (a great fall at once) and our weekly Gazets did some Months past inform us, that the Sweeds by a Law had brought down their Interest to 6 per cent; neither of which can have any good effects upon us, but certainly the contrary, except by way of emulation they quicken us to provide in time for our own Good and Prosperity.

I have now done with this Controversie, and therein discharge my Duty to my native Country, and though Ignorance, Malice, or private Interest may yet for some time oppose it; I am confident the Wisdom of my Country-men, will at length find their true and general Interest, in the Establishment of such a Law, which as to my own particular concernments, signifies not two Farthings whether they do or not.

A DISCOURSE ABOUT TRADE

TRADE AND INTEREST OF MONEY CONSIDERED, &c.

CHAP. II.

Concerning the Relief and Employment of the Poor.

TRADE AND INTEREST OF MONEY CONSIDERED, &c.

CHAP. II.

Concerning the Relief and Employment of the Poor.

This is a calm Subject, and thwarts no common or private Interest amongst us, except that of the common Enemy of Mankind (the Devil) so I hope that what shall be offered towards the effecting of so universally acceptable a Work as this, and the removal of the innumerable Inconveniences that do now and have in all Ages attended this Kingdom, through defect of such provision for the Poor, will not be ill taken, although the Plaister at first essay do not exactly fit the Sore.

In the Discourse of this subject, I shall first assert some particulars, which I think are agreed by common Consent, and from thence take occasion to proceed to what is more doubtful.

1. That our Poor in England have always been in a most sad and wretched condition, some Famished for want of Bread, others starved with Cold and Nakedness, and many whole Families in all the out Parts of Cities and great Towns, commonly remain in a languishing, nasty and useless Condition, Uncomfortable to themselves, and Unprofitable to

the Kingdom, this is confessed and lamented by all Men.

2. That the Children of our Poor bred up in Beggery and Laziness, do by that means become not only of unhealthy Bodies, and more then ordinarily subject to many loathsome Diseases, whereof very many die in their tender Age; and if any of them do arrive to years and strength, they are by their idle habits contracted in their Youth, rendered for ever after indisposed to Labour, and serve only to stock the Kingdom with Thieves and Beggars.

3. That if all our impotent Poor were provided for, and those of both Sexes and all Ages that can do Work of any kind, employed, it would redound some Hundreds of Thousands of Pounds per annum to the publick Advantage.

4. That it is our Duty to God and Nature, so to Provide for, and Employ the Poor.

5. That by so doing one of the great Sins (for which this Land ought to mourn) would be removed.

6. That our fore-Fathers had pious Intentions towards this good Work, as appears by the many Statutes made by them to this purpose.

7. That there are places in the World, wherein the Poor are so provided for, and employed, as in Holland, Hambrough, New-England and others, and as I am informed now in the City of Paris.

Thus far we all agree: The first Question then that naturally occurs, is,

Question, How comes it to pass that in England we do not, nor ever did comfortably Maintain and Employ our Poor?

The common Answers to this Question are, two.

1. That our Laws to this purpose are as good as any in the World, but we fail in the execution.

2. That formerly in the days of our pious Ancestors the work was done, but now Charity is deceased, and that is the reason

we see the Poor so neglected as now they are.

In both which Answers (I humbly conceive) the Effect is mistaken for the Cause: For though it cannot be denied, but there hath been, and is a great failure in the Execution of those Statutes which relate to the Poor; yet I say, the cause of that failure, hath been occasioned by defect of the Laws themselves.

For otherwise, what is the reason that in our late times of Confusion and Alteration, wherein almost every Party, in the Nation, at one time or other, took their turn at the Helm, and all had that Compass (those Laws) to Stear by, and yet none of them could, or ever did, conduct the Poor into a Harbour of security to them, and profit to the Kingdom, i. e. none sufficiently maintained the Impotent, and employed the Indigent amongst us: And if this was never done in any Age, nor by any sort of Men whatsoever in this Kingdom, who had the use of those Laws now in force, it seems to me a very strong Argument that it never could, nor ever will be done by those Laws, and that consequently the defect lies in the Laws themselves, not in the Men, i. e. those that should put them in Execution.

As to the second Answer to the aforesaid Question, wherein want of Charity is assigned for another cause why the Poor are now so much neglected, I think it is a scandalous ungrounded Accusation of our Contemporaries (except in relation to Building of Churches, which I confess this Generation is not so prophense to as former have been) for most that I converss with, are not so much troubled to part with their Money, as how to place it, that it may do good, and not hurt to the Kingdom: For, if they give to the Beggars in the Streets, or at their Doors, they fear they may do hurt by encouraging that Lazy Unprofitable kind of Life; and if they give more then their Proportions in their respective Parishes, that (they say) is but giving to the Rich, for the Poor are not set on Work thereby, nor have the more given them; but only their Rich Neighbours pay the less. And for what was given in Churches to the visited Poor, and to such as were impoverished by the Fire; we have heard of so many and great Abuses of that kind of Charity, that most Men are under sad discouragements in relation thereunto.

I write not this to divert any Man from Works of Charity of any kind: He that gives to any in Want does well; but he that gives to Employ and Educate the Poor, so as to render them useful to the Kingdom, in my judgment does better.

And here by the way, not to leave Men at a loss how to dispose of what God shall incline their Hearts to give for the Benefit of the Poor, I think it not Impertinent to propose the Hospitals of this City, and Poor Labouring People that have many Children, and make a hard shift to sustain them by their Industery, whereof there are multitudes in the out Parts of this City, as the best Objects of Charity at present.

But to return to my purpose, viz. to prove that the want of Charity likewise that is now, and always hath been, in relation to the Poor, proceeds from a defect in our Laws. Ask any Charitable minded Man as he goes along the Streets of London, viewing the Poor, viz. Boyes, Girles, Men and Women of all Ages, and many in good Health, &c. why he and others do not take care for the setting those poor Creatures to Work? Will he not readily answer, that he wisheth heartily it could be done, though it cost him a great part of his Estate, but he is but one Man, and can do nothing towards it, giving them Money, as hath been said, being but to bring them into a liking and continuance in that way.

The second Question then is,

Question 2. Wherein lies the defect of our present Laws relating to the Poor?

I answer, that there may be many, but I shall here take notice of one only, which I think to be Fundamental, and which until altered, the Poor in England can never be well Provided for, or Employed; and that when the said fundamental Error is well amended, it is almost impossible they should lack either Work or Maintenance.

The said radical Error I esteem to be the leaving it to the care of every Parish to Maintain their own Poor only; upon which follows the shifting off, sending or whiping back the poor Wanderers to the Place of their Birth, or last Abode; the practice whereof I have seen many years in London, to signifie as much as ever it will, which is just nothing of good to the Kingdom in general, or the Poor thereof, though it be sometimes by accident to some of them a Punishment without effect; I say without effect, because it reforms not the Party, nor desposeth the minds of others to Obedience, which are the true ends of all Punishment.

As for instance, a poor idle Person, that will not Work, or that no Body will Employ in the Country, comes up to London to set up the Trade of Begging, such a person probably may Begg up and down the Streets seven years, it may be seven and twenty, before any Body asketh why she doth so, and if at length she hath the ill hap in some Parish, to meet with a more vigilant Beadle then one of twenty of them are, all he does is but to lead her the length of five or six Houses into another Parish, and then concludes, as his Masters the Parishioners do, that he hath done the part of a most diligent Officer: But suppose he should yet go further to the end of his Line, which is the end of the Law; and the perfect Execution of his Office; that is, suppose he should carry this poor wretch to a Justice of the Peace, and he should order the Delinquent to be Whipt and sent from Parish to Parish, to the place of her Birth or last Abode, which not one Justice of twenty (through pitty or other cause) will do; even this is a great charge upon the Country, and yet the business of the Nation it self wholly undone: for no sooner doth the Delinquent arrive at the place assigned, but for Shame or Idleness she presently deserts it, and wanders directly back, or some other way, hoping for better Fortune, whilst the Parish to which she is sent, knowing her a Lazy and perhaps a worse qualited person, is as willing to be rid of her, as she is to be gone from thence.

If it be here retorted upon me, that by my own confession, much of this mischief happens by the non, or ill Execution of the Laws, I say, better Execution then you have seen you must not expect; and there was never a good Law made that was not well executed, the fault of the Law causing a failure of execution, it being natural to all Men to use the remedy next at hand, and rest satisfied with shifting the Evil from their own Doors; which in regard they can so easily do, by threatning or thrusting a poor Body out of the verge of their own Parish, it is unreasonable and vain to hope that ever it will be otherwise.

For the Laws against Inmates, and empowering the Parishioners to take Security before they suffer any poor Person to Inhabit amongst them; it may be they were prudent constitutions at the times they were made (and before England was a place of Trade) and may be so still in some Countries, but I am sure in Cities and great Towns of Trade they are altogether improper, and contrary to the practice of other Cities and Trading Towns abroad. The Riches of a City, as of a Nation, consisting in the multitude of Inhabitants; and if so, you must allow Inmates, or have a City of Cottages. And if a right course be taken for the Sustentation of the Poor, and setting them on Work, you need invent no Stratagems to keep them out, but rather to bring them in. For the resort of Poor to a City or Nation well managed, is in effect, the conflux of Riches to that City or Nation; and therefore the subtil Dutch receive, and relieve, or employ all that come to them, not enquiring what Nation, much less what Parish they are of.

Question, 3. The third Question: If the defect be in our Laws, how shall we find a remedy that may be rational and consistent?

This I confess is a hard and difficult question, it is one of the Ardua Regni, and may very well deserve the most deliberate consideration of our wisest Counsellors. And if a whole Session of Parliament were employed on this singular concern, I think it would be time spent as much to the glory of God and good of this Nation, as in any thing that noble and worthy Patriots of their Country can be engaged in: But seeing I have adventured thus far, I shall humbly proceed to offer some general proposals that have a tendency towards the effecting this great Work, which being seriously thought of and debated by wiser men, may be capable of such melioration as may render them in a great measure effectual to the Kingdom in general, although at present, to prevent that common Objection, that great Mutations are dangerous; I shall only propose them to be experimented in these parts of the Kingdom, which are the Vitals of our body politick, which being once made sound, the care of the rest will not be difficult.

Proposition, 1. First then I propose, That the City of London and Westminster, Burrough of Southwark, and all other places within the usual Lines of Communication, described in the weekly Bills of Mortality, may by Act of Parliament be associated into one Province or Line of Communication for relief of the Poor.

2. That there be one Assembly of men (and such as they shall from time to time appoint and deputise) entrusted with the care for, and treasure of all the Poor within the said Pale or Line of Communication.

3. That the said Assembly be incorporated by Act of Parliament, with perpetual Succession, by the name of Fathers of the Poor, or some other honourable and significant Title.

4. That all Constables, Church-wardens, Overseers, or other Officers in all Parishes, within the said Line, be subordinate and accomptable to the said Fathers of the Poor, and their Deputies for, and in all things relating to the Poor.

5. That the said Fathers of the Poor may have liberty to assess and receive into their common Treasury, for relief of their Poor, so much Money from every Parish as they yearly paid to that purpose any of the three Years preceding this Constitution, and to compel the Payment thereof, but not of more.

6. That the said Fathers of the Poor, and their Deputies, may have very large and sufficient power in all things relating to the Poor, and particularly to have and receive the charitable benevolence of all Persons once every Lord's Day in every Parish-Church, and in any other Meeting of Pious Christians, and at any other time or times which they shall think fit.

7. That the said Fathers of the Poor, and such as they shall authorize, may have power to purchase Lands, erect and endow Work-houses, Hospitals, and Houses of Correction, and to exercise all other Powers relating to the Poor, that any number of Justices of the Peace now may do, in their Quarter-Sessions or otherwise.

8. That the said Fathers of the Poor may have Power to send such Poor beyond the Seas as they shall think fit into his Majesties Plantations, taking Security for their comfortable Maintenance during their Service, and for their freedom afterwards.

9. That the said Fathers of the Poor may have Power to erect petty Bancks and Lumbards for the benefit of the Poor, if they shall find it convenient, and also to receive the one half of what is paid at all the Doors of Play-Houses, and have the Patent for Farthings, and to do whatever else his Majesty and the Parliament shall think fit to recommend to them, or leave to their discretion.

10. That the Treasure that shall be collected for this purpose be accounted sacred, and that it be Felony to misapply, conceal, lend or convert it to any other use or purpose whatsoever.

11. That there be no Oaths, or other Tests imposed upon the said Fathers of the Poor, at their admission, to bar our Nonconformists, amongst whom there will be found some excellent Instruments for this good Work, and such as will constantly attend it (for if they be kept out, the People will be cold in their Charity, and in their hopes of the success.)

12. That the said Fathers of the Poor may constantly wear some honourable Meddal, such as the King and Parliament shall devise, besides the green Staff which is now used in London to such like purpose (but upon extraordinary dayes only) to denote their Authority and Office, at all times, and in all places, after the manner of the Habits in Spain, or rather, as have all the Familiars of the Inquisition in most Romish Countries, with admirable effect, though to a wicked purpose; the consequence whereof will be, that the said Fathers of the Poor, being numerous, and disperst by their Habitations and Business, into most parts of their Province, will readily see any neglects of Officers, and as easily redress them; the Meddal which they wear about them, being a sufficient Warrant to command Obedience from all Parish Officers where-ever they come, although their Persons be not known there.

13. That the said Fathers of the Poor may have liberty to admit into their Society and all Powers and Priviledges equal with them, any Persons that are willing to serve God, their King and Country in this pious and publick Work, the Persons desiring to be so admitted, paying at their admission 100 l. or more into the Poors Treasury, as a demonstration of the Sincerity of their Intentions to labour in and cultivate this most Religious Vineyard. This I only offer because the number of the said Fathers of the Poor hereafter mentioned, may be

thought rather too few then too many.

14. That the said Fathers of the Poor, besides the Authority now exercised by Justices of the Peace, may have some less limitted Powers given them, in relation to the punishment of their own, and Parish Officers by pecuniary mulcts for the Poors benefit in case of neglect, and otherwise as his Majesty, and the Parliament shall think fit.

15. That the said Fathers of the Poor may have freedom to set the Poor on work about whatsoever Manufacture they think fit, with a Non obstante to all Patents that have been or shall be granted to any private Person or Persons for the sole Manufacture of any Commodity, the want of which priviledge, I have been told, was a prejudice to the Work-house at Clerkenwell, in their late design of setting their poor Children about making of Hangings.

16. That all Vacancies by reason of death of any of the said Fathers of the Poor be perpetually supplied by election of the Survivors.

Quest. 4. The fourth Question is, who shall be the Persons entrusted with so great a Work, and such excess of Power?

This is a Question likewise of some difficulty, and the more in regard of our present Differences in Religion, but I shall answer it as well as I can.

In general I say, They must be such as the People must have ample satisfaction in, or else the whole Design will be lost: For if the universality of the People be not satisfied with the Persons, they will never part with their Money; but if they be well satisfied therein, they will be miraculously charitable.

Quest. 5. This begets a fifth Question, viz. What sort of men the people will be most satisfied in?

I answer, I think in none so well as such only as a common Hall of the Livery-men of London shall make choice of, it being evident by the experience of many Ages, that the several

Corporations in London are the best Administrators of what is left to charitable Uses, that have ever been in this Kingdom, which is manifest in the regular, just and prudent management of the Hospitals of London, and was wisely observed by Doctor Collet Dean of St Paul's that prudent Ecclesiastick, when he left the Government of that School, and other great Revenues assigned by him for charitable Uses, unto the disposition of the Mercers Company.

Object. But here it may be objected, That Country-Gentlemen, who have power in places of their Residences, and pay out of their large Estates considerable sums towards the Maintenance of their Poor within the aforelimited Precincts, may be justly offended if they likewise have not a share in the distribution of what shall be raised to that purpose.

Answ. I answer the force of this objection may be much taken off if the City be obliged to choose but a certain number out of the City, as suppose seventy for London, ten out of Southwark for that Burrough, twenty for Westminster, this would best satisfie the People, & I think do the work: But if it be thought too much for the City to have the choice of any more then their own seventy, the Justices of Peace in their Quarter-Sessions may nominate and appoint their own number of Persons to assist for their respective Jurisdictions, and so to supply the vacancy in case of Death, &c. But all must be conjunctive, but one Body politick, or the work will never be done.

Quest. 6. The sixth Question is, What will be the advantage to the Kingdom in general, and to the Poor in particular, that will accrue by such a Society of men, more than is enjoyed by the Laws at present?

I answer; Innumerable and unspeakable are the Benefits to this Kingdom that will arise from the Consultations and Debates of such a wise and honest Council, who being men so elected as aforesaid, will certainly conscionably study and labour to discharge their trust in this service of God, their King and Country.

1st, The Poor, of what quality soever, as soon as they are met with, will be immediately relieved or set on work where they are found, without hurrying them from place to place, and torturing their Bodies to no purpose.

2. Charitable-minded-men will know certainly where to dispose of their Charity, so as it may be employed to right purposes.

3. House-keepers will be freed from the intolerable incumbrance of Beggars at their Doors.

4. The Plantations will be regularly supplied with Servants, and those that are send thither well provided for.

5. The said Assembly will doubtless appoint some of their own Members to visit and relieve such as are sick, as often as there shall be occasion, together with poor labouring Families both in City and Suburbs.

6. Poor Children will be instructed in Learning and Arts, and thereby rendred serviceable to their Country, and many other worthy Acts done for publick good by the joynt delibaration of so many prudent and pious men, assisted with such a Power and Purse, more then can be fore-seen or expressed by a private Person.

Quest. 7. The seventh Question may be, What shall all the Poor of these Cities and Countries, being very numerous, be employed about!

This question will be answer'd best by the said Assembly themselves when they have met and consulted together, who cannot be presumed defficient of Invention to set all the Poor on work, especially since they may easily have admirable Presidents from the practice of Holland in this particular, and have already very good ones of their own, in the orders of their Hospitals of Christ-Church and Bridewell in London; the Girles may he employed in mending the Clothes of of the Aged, in Spinning, Carding and other linnen Manufactures, and many in Sowing Linnen for the Exchange, on any Housekeepers that will put out Linnen to the Matrons that have the Government of them.

The Boys in picking Okam, making Pins, rasping Wood, making Hangings, or any other Manufacture of any kind, which whether it turns to present profit or not, is not much material, the great Business of the Nation being first but to keep the Poor from Begging and Starving, and enuring such as are able to Labour and Discipline, that they may be hereafter useful Members to the Kingdom: But to conclude, I say the wisest Man living, solitarily cannot propose or imagine such excellent ways and methods as will be invented by the united Wisdom of so grave an Assembly.

The sitting of the said Assembly I humbly conceive, ought to be, De die in diem; the Quorum not more then thirteen; whether they shall Yearly, Monthly or Weekly choose a President, how they shall distribute themselves into the several quarters of the Communication, what Treasurers and other Officers to employ, and where, and how many, will best be determined by themselves, and that without difficulty, because many that will probably be Members of the said Assembly, have already had large experience of the Government of the Hospitals of London: The manner of Election of the said Fathers of the Poor, I humbly suppose, cannot possibly be better contrived, then after the same way which the East-India-Company choose their Committee, which will prevent the Confusion, Irregularity and Incertitude that may attend the Election of Voices, or holding up of Hands; especially because the persons to be elected at one time will be very many; the said manner proposed is, every Elector, viz. every Livery-Man to bring to Guild-Hall at the appointed day for Elections, a List of the whole number of Persons, such as he thinks fit that are to be Elected, and deliver the same openly unto such Persons as the Lord Mayor, Aldermen and Common-Council-Men shall appoint to make the Scrutiney; which Persons so entrusted, with the said Scrutiney, seven, or ten days after, as shall be thought fit, at another common Hall may declare who are the Persons Elected by the Majority of Votes.

If it be here objected to the whole purpose of this Treatise, that this work may as well be done in distinct Parishes, if all Parishes were obliged to Build Work-Houses, and Employ their Poor therein; as Dorchester and some others have done with good success.

I answer, that such attempts have been made in many places to my knowledge, with very good intents and strenuons endeavours, but all that ever I heard of, proved vain and ineffectual, as I fear will that of Clerken-Well, except that single instance of the Town of Dorchester, which yet signifies nothing in relation to the Kingdom in general, because all other places cannot do the like, nor doth the Town of Dorchester entertain any but their own Poor only, and Whip away all others; whereas that which I design is to propose such a Foundation, as shall be large, wise, honest and rich enough to maintain and employ all Poor that come within the Pale of their Communication, without enquiring where they were Born, or last Inhabited: Which I dare affirm with Humility, that nothing but a National, or at least such a Provincial Purse can so well do, nor any persons in this Kingdom, but such only as shall be pickt out by popular Election for the reason before alledged, viz. That in my opinion, three fourths at least of the Stock must issue from the Charity of the people; as I doubt not but it will to a greater proportion, if they be satisfied in the Managers thereof; But if otherwise, not the fortieth; I might say not the hundredth part.

I propose the Majority of the said Fathers of the Poor to be Citizens (though I am none my self) because I think a great share of the Money to be employed, must and will come from them, if ever the Work be well done, as also, because their Habitations are nearest the Center of their Business, and they best acquainted with all affairs of this nature, by their experience in the Government of the Hospitals.

Earnestly to desire and endeavour, that the Poor of England should be better provided for and employed, is a work that was much studdied by my deceased Father, and therefore though I be as ready to confess, as any shall be to charge me with Disability to propose a Model of Laws for this great Affair, yet I hope the more Ingenuous will pardon me for endeavouring to give aim towards it, since it is so much my Duty, which in this particular I shall be careful to perform (though I may be too remise in others) as shall appear by more visible and apparent demonstrations, if ever this design, or any other (that is like to effect what is desired) succeed.

Now I have adventured thus far, I shall proceed to publish my Thoughts and Observations concerning some other things that have relation to Trade, which I do without any purpose or design, save only to give occasion to my Country-men, to be Discoursing and Meditating upon those things which have a tendancy to publick Good, from whence (though my Suggestions should be mistakes) probably some good effect may ensue, and therefore the Ingenuous, I know, though they may differ from me, will not blame me for the attempt.

A DISCOURSE ABOUT TRADE

TRADE AND INTEREST OF MONEY CONSIDERED, &c.

CHAP. III.

Concerning Companies of Merchants.

TRADE AND INTEREST OF MONEY CONSIDERED, &c.

CHAP. III.

Concerning Companies of Merchants.

Companies of Merchants are of two sorts, viz. Companies in joynt Stock, such as the East-India-Company, the Morea-Company (which is a Branch of the Turkey-Company) and the Greenland-Company, which is a Branch of the Muscovia-Company; the other sort are Companies who trade not by a joynt Stock ,but only are under a Government and Regulation, such are the Hambrough-Company, the Turkey-Company, the Eastland-Company, the Muscovia-Company.

It hath for many Years been a moote case, whether any Encorporating of Merchants, be for publik Good or not.

For my own part I am of Opinion.

That for Countries with which his Majesty hath no Allieance, nor can have any by reason of their distance, or Barbarity, or non-Communication with the Princes of Christendom, &c. where there is a necessity of Maintaining Forces and Forts, (such as East-India and Guinia) Companies of Merchants are absolute necessary.

2. It seems evident to me, that the greatest part of these two Trades ought for publick Good, to be managed by joynt Stock.

3. It's questionable to me, whether any other Company of Merchants are for publick good or hurt.

4. I conclude however, that all restrictions of Trade are naught, and consequently that no Company whatsoever, whether they Trade in a joynt Stock or under Regulation, can be for publick Good, except it may be easie for all, or any of his Majesty's Subjects to be admitted into all, or any of the said Companies, at any time for a very inconsiderable Fine, and that if the Fine exceed 20 l. including all Charges of admission, it is too much, and that for these Reasons.

1. Because the Dutch who thrive best by Trade, and have the surest rules to thrive by, admit not only any of their own People, but even Jews and all kind of Aliens, to be Free of any of their Societies of Merchants, or any of their Cities or Towns Corporate.

2. Nothing in the World can enable us to coape with the Dutch in any Trade, but encrease of Hands and Stock, which a general admission will do; many Hands and much Stock being as necessary to the Prosperity of any Trade, as Men and Money to warfare.

3. There is no pretence of any good to the Nation by Companies, but only Order and Regulation of Trade; and if that be preserved (which the admission of all that will come in and submit to the Regulation, will not prejudice) all the good to the Nation that can be hoped for by Companies, is obtained.

4. The Eastland, besides our Native Commodities, spend great quantities of Italian, Spanish, Portugal and French Commodities, viz. Oyle, Wine, Fruit, Sugar, Succads, Shoomack, &c. Now, in regard our East-Country Merchants of England are few, compared with the Dutch, and intend principally that one Trade out and home, and consequently are

not so conversant in the aforesaid Commodities, nor forward to adventure upon them, and seeing that by the Companies Charter our Italian, Spanish, Portugal and French Merchants, who understand those Commodities perfectly well, are excluded those Trades, or at least, if the Company will give them leave to send out those Goods, are not permitted to bring in the Returns; it follows, that the Dutch must supply Denmark, Sweeden, and all parts of the Baltique, with most of those Commodities, and so it is in fact.

5. The Dutch who have no Eastland-Companies, yet have ten times the Trade to the Eastern parts as we have; and for Italy, Spain and Portugal, where we have no Companies, we have yet left full as much, if not more Trade, then the Dutch. And for Russia and Greenland where we have Companies (and I think Establisht by Act or Acts of Parliament) our Trade is in effect wholly lost, while the Dutch, have, without Companies, encreased theirs to above forty times the the Bulk of what the residue of ours now is.

From whence may be inferred.

1. That restrained limitted Companies are not alone sufficient to preserve and encrease a Trade.

2. That limitted Companies, though Established by Act of Parliament, may lo se a Trade.

3. That Trade may be carried on to any part of Christendom, and encreased without Companies.

4. That we have declined more, at least have encreasedless, in those Trades limitted to Companies, then in others where all his Majesties Subjects have had equal freedom to Trade.

The common Objections against this easie admission of all his Majesties Subjects into Companies of Merchants, are;

Object. 1. If all persons may come into any Company of Merchants on such easie terms, then young Gentlemen, Shop-keepers and divers others will turn Merchants, who through their own unskilfulness will pay dear for our native Commodities here, and sell them cheap abroad; and also buy Foreign Commodities dear abroad, and sell them here for less then their cost, to the Ruin of themselves, and Destruction of Trade.

I answer, first, caveat emptor, let particular Men look to themselves, and so doubtless they will in those Trades for which there are now Companies, as well as they do in others for which there are no Companies.

It is the care of Law-makers first and principally, to provide for the People in gross, not particulars, and if the consequence of so easie an admission, should be to make our Manufactures cheap abroad, and Foreign Commodities cheap here, (as is alledged) our Nation in general would have the advantage both ways.

Object. 2. If all should be admitted, &c. Shop-keepers, being the Retailors, of the same Commodities the Company Imports, would have so much the advantage of the Merchant, that he would beat the Merchant wholly out of the Trade.

I answer, first, We see no such thing in Holland, nor in the open Trades, viz. France, Spain, Portugal, Italy, and all our own Plantations, neither can that well be, for to drive a retail Trade to any purpose, requires a Mans full Stock, as well as his full attendance, and so doth it to drive the Trade of a Merchant, and therefore few can find Stock and time to attend both; from whence it follows, that of the many Hundreds which in memory have turned Merchants, very few continued long to follow both, but commonly after two or three Years Experience, betake themselves wholly to Merchandizing, or returned to the sole Exercise of their Retail way; but whether they do, or do not, concerns not the Nation in general, whose common Interest is to buy cheap, whatever appellation the Seller hath, whether that of a meer Merchant, Gentleman, or a

Shop-keeper.

Object. 3. If Shop-keepers and other unexperienced persons may turn Merchants, &c. they will through Ignorance neglect buying and sending out our Native Manufactures, and will send out our Money, or Bills of Exchange to buy Foreign Commodities, which is an apparent National loss.

I answer, that Shop-keepers are, like all other Men (led by their profit) and if it be for their Advantage to send out Manufactures, they will do it without forcing; and if it be for their Profit to send over Money or Bills of Exchange, they will do that, and so will Merchants as soon and as much as they.

Object. 4. If any may be admitted, &c. what do we get by our seven Years Service, and the great Sums of Money our Parents gave to bind us Apprentices to Merchants? &c. And who will hereafter bind his Son to a Merchant?

I answer, The end of Service and giving of Money with Apprentices, I have always understood to be the Learning of the Art or Science of Merchandizing, not the purchasing of an Immunity or Monopoly to the prejudice of our Country; and that it is so, is evident from the practice, there being many general Merchants that are free of no particular Company, who can have as large Sums of Money with Apprentices, as any other that are free of one or more particular Companies of Merchants; and many Merchants that are free of particular Companies, unto whom few will give any considerable sums of Money with Apprentices; the proportion of Money given with Apprentices not following the Company a Merchant is free of, but the condition the Master, as to his more or less reputed skill in his Calling, Thriving or going backward, greater or lesser Trade, well or ill Government of himself and Family, &c.

Obj. 5. If all should be admitted on such easie terms, will not that be manifest Injustice to the Companies of Merchants, who by themselves or Predecessors have been at great Disburstments to purchase Priviledges & Immunities abroad, as the Turkey-Company, and the Hambrough-Company have done.

I answer, That I am yet to learn that any Company of Merchants not trading with a joynt Stock, such as the Turkey, Hambrough, Muscovia and Eastland Companies ever purchased their Priviledges, or built and maintained Forts, Castles or Factories, or made any Wars at their own charge; but I know the Turkey Company do maintain an Embassador and two Consuls, and are sometimes necessitated to make Presents to the Grand Senior, or his great Officers; and the Hambrough Company are at some charge to maintain their Deputy, and Minister at Hambrough; and I think it would be great Injustice that any should trade to the places within their Charters, without paying the same Duties or Leviations towards the Companies charge as the present Adventurers do pay, but I know not why any should be barred from trading to those places, or forced to pay a great Fine for admition, that are willing to pay the Companies Duties, and submit to the Companies regulation and orders in other respects.

Obj. 6. If all may be admitted as aforesaid, then such numbers of Shop-keepers and others would come into the Society of Merchants, as would by the Majority of Votes so much alter the Governours, Deputy and Assistants of the respective Companies, that Ignorant Persons would come into those ruling places, to the general prejudice of those Trades.

I answer, Those that make this Objection, if they be Merchants, know there is very little in it, for that it is not to be expected that twenty Shop-keepers will come into any one Company in a Year; and therefore can have no considerable influence upon the Elections; but if many more should come in, it would be the better for the Nation, and not the worse for the Company, for that all men are lead by their Interest, and it being the common Interest of all that engage in any

Trade, that the Trade should be regulated and governed by wise, honest and able men, there is no doubt but most men will Vote for such as they esteem so to be, which is manifest in the East-India-Company, where neither Gentlemen nor Shop-keepers were at first excluded, neither are they yet kept out; any English-man whatsoever being permitted to come into that Company that will buy an Action, paying only five Pounds to the Company for his admission; and yet undeniable experience hath convinced all Gain-sayers in this matter; that Company, since its having had so large and National a Foundation, having likewise had a succession of much better Governours, Deputies and Assistants then ever it had upon that narrow bottom it stood formerly, when none could be admitted to the freedom of that Company, for less than a Fine of Fifty Pounds; and the success hath been answerable, For the first Company settled upon that narrow limitted Interest, although their Stock was larger, then this, decayed and finally came to ruin and destruction; Whereas on the contrary, this being settled on more rational, and consequently more just, as well as more profitable Principles, hath through Gods Goodness thriven and encreased to the trebling of their first Stock.

A DISCOURSE ABOUT TRADE

TRADE AND INTEREST OF MONEY CONSIDERED, &c.

CHAP. IV.

Concerning the Act of Navigation.

TRADE AND INTEREST OF MONEY CONSIDERED, &c.

CHAP. IV.

Concerning the Act of Navigation.

Though this Act be by most concluded a very beneficial Act for this Kingdom, especially by the Masters and Owners of Shiping, and by all Sea-men; yet some there are, both wise and honest Gentlemen and Merchants, that doubt whether the Inconveniencies it hath brought with it, be not greater then the Conveniencies.

For my own part, I am of Opinion that in relation to Trade, Shiping, Profit and Power, it is one of the choicest and most prudent Acts that ever was made in England, and without which we had not now been Owners of one half of the Shiping, nor Trade, nor employed one half of the Sea-men which we do at present; but seeing time hath discovered some Inconveniencies in it, if not Defects, which in my poor opinion do admit of an easie Amendment, and seeing that the whole Act is not approved by unanimous consent, I thought fit to discourse a little concerning it, wherein, after my plain method I shall lay down such Objections as I have met with, and subjoyn my Answers, with such Reasons as occur to my memory in confirmation of my own Opinion.

The Objections against the whole Act are such as these;

Object. 1. Some have told me, That I on all occasions magnifie the Dutch policy in relation to their Trade, and the Dutch have no Act of Navigation, and therefore they are certainly not always in the right, as to the understanding of their true Interest in Trade, or else we are in the wrong in this.

I answer, I am yet to be informed where the Dutch have missed their proper Interest in Trade, but that which is fit for one Nation to do in relation to their Trade, is not fit for all, no more then the same Policy is necessary to a prevailing Army that are Masters of the Field, to an Army of less force, then to be able to encounter their Enemy at all times and places: The Dutch by reason of their great Stocks, low Interest, multitude of Merchants and Shiping, are Masters of the Field in Trade, and therefore have no need to build Castles, Fortresses and places of Retreat; such I account Laws of limitation, and securing of particular Trades to the Natives of any Kingdom; because they, viz. the Dutch, may be well assured, That no Nation can enter in common with them in any Trade, to gain Bread by it, while their own use of Money is at 3 per Cent, and others at 6 per Cent and upwards, &c. Whereas if we should suffer their Shiping in common with ours in those Trades, which are secured to the English by Act of Navigation, they must necessarily in a few Years, for the Reasons above-said, eat us quite out of them.

Object. 2. The second Objection to the whole Act is; Some will confess that as to Merchants and Owners of Ships the Act of Navigation is eminently beneficial, but say, that Merchants and Owners are but an inconsiderable number of men in respect of the whole Nation, and that Interest of the greater number, that our Native Commodities and Manufactures should be taken from us at the best rates, and foreign Commodities sold us at the cheapest, with admission of Dutch Merchants and Shiping in common with the English, by my own implication would effect.

My answer is, That I cannot deny but this may be true, if the present profit of the generality be barely and singly considered; but this Kingdom being an Island, the defence whereof hath alwayes been our Shiping and Sea-men, it seems to me absolutely necessary that Profit and Power ought joyntly to be considered, and if so, I think none can deny but the Act of Navigation hath and doth occasion building and employing of three times the number of Ships and Sea-men, that otherwise we should or would do, and that consequently, If our Force at Sea were so greatly impared, it would expose us to the receiving of all kind of Injuries and Affronts from our Neighbours, and in conclusion render us a despicable and miserable People.

Objections to several Parts of the Act of Navigation.

Object. 1. The Inhabitants and Planters of our Plantations in America, say, This Act will in time ruin their Plantations, if they may not be permitted, at least to carry their Sugars to the best Markets, and not be compell'd to send all to, and receive all Commodities from England.

I answer, If they were not kept to the Rules of the Act of Navigation, the consequence would be, that in a few Years the benefit of them would be wholly lost to the Nation; it being agreeable to the Policy of the Dutch, Danes, French, Spaniards, Portugals, and all Nations in the World, to keep their external Provinces and Colonies in a subjection unto, and dependency upon their Mother-Kingdom; and if they should not do so, the Dutch, who as I have said, are Masters of the Field in Trade, would carry away the greatest of advantage by the Plantations, of all the Princes in Christendom, leaving us and others only the trouble of breeding men, and sending them abroad to cultivate the Ground, and have Bread for their Industry.

Here by the way, with entire submission to the greater Wisdom of those whom it much more concerns, give me leave to Query, Whether, instead of the late prohibition of Irish Cattle, it would not have been more for the benefit of this Kingdom of England, to suffer the Irish to bring into England not only their live Cattle, but also all other Commodities of the Growth or Manufacture of that Kingdom, Custom free, or on easie Customs, and to prohibit them from Trading homeward or outward with the Dutch, or our own Plantations, or any other places, except the Kingdom of England? Most certainly such a Law would in a few Years wonderfully encrease the Trade, Shiping and Riches of this Nation.

Query 2. Would not this be a good addition to the Act of Navigation, and much encrease the employment of English Shiping and Sea-men, as well in bringing from thence all the Commodities of that Country, as supplying that Country with Deals, Salt, and all other foreign Commodities which now they have from the Dutch?

Que. 3. Would not this be a means effectually to prevent the Exportation of Irish Wool, which now goes frequently into France and Holland, to the manifest and great damage both of England and Ireland?

Que 4. Would not this be a Fortress or Law to secure to us the whole Trade of Ireland?

Que. 5. Would not this render that which now diminisheth, and seems dangerous to the value of Lands in England, viz. the growth of Ireland advantagious, by encrease of Trade and Shiping, and consequently the power of this Kingdom?

Object. 2. The second Ojection to part of the Act of Navigation, is usually made by the Eastland and Norway Merchants, who affirm, that in effect their Trade is much declined since the passing the Act of Navigation; and the Danes, Sweeds, Holsteners, and all Easterlings, who by the said Act may Import Timber, and other Eastern Commodities, have encreased in the number of their Shiping, imployed in this Trade, since our Act of Navigation, at least two third parts; and the English have proportionably declined in the number of theirs imployed in that Trade.

I answer, That I believe the matter of Fact asserted is true, as well as the cause assigned, viz. the Act of Navigation; and yet this should not make us out of love with that excellent Law, rather let it put us upon contriving the Amendment of this seeming Defect, or Inconvenience, the Cure whereof, I hope, upon mature consideration, will not be found difficult, for which I humbly propound to the Wisdom of Parliament, viz. That a Law be made to impose a Custom of at least 50l. per Cent on all Eastland Commodities, Timber, Boards, Pipe-Staves and Salt imported into England and Ireland upon any Ships but English built Ships; or at least such only as are sailed with an English Master, and at least three fourths English Marriners.

And that for these Reasons;

Reas. First, If this be not done, the Danes, Sweedes and Easterlings will certainly in a few Years carry the whole Trade, by reason of the difference of the charge of building a Ship fit for that Trade there or here, viz. a Fly-boat of 300 Tuns new built, and set to Sea for such a Voyage, may cost there 13 or 1400l. which here would cost from 22 to 2400 l. which is so vast a disproportion, that it is impossible for an English man to coape with a Dane in that Navigation under such a discouragement; to ballance which there is nothing but the Strangers duty which the Dane now pays, which may come to 5 or 6 l per Ship per Voyage at most, one with another, which is incompitable with the difference of Price between the first cost of the Ships in either Nation: And this is so evident to those who are conversant in those Trades, that besides the decrease of our Shiping and encrease of theirs that hath already happened, ours in probability had been wholly beaten out of the Trade, and only Danes and Easterlings freighted, had we been necessitated to build English Ships, and had not been recruited on moderate Prices by Fly-boats (being Ships proper for this Trade) taken in the late Dutch War, and by a further supply of Scotch Prizes likewise, through his Majesties permission and indulgence.

Reas. 2. Because the number of Strangers Ships imployed in the aforesaid Trade yearly, I estimtae to be about two hundred Sail; which if such a Law were made, must unavoidably be all excluded, and the Employment fall wholly into English Hands; which would be an excellent Nursery, and give constant Maintenance to a brave number of English Sea-men, more then we can or do employ at present.

Reas. 3. The Act of Navigation is now of seventeen or eighteen Years standing in England, and yet in all these Years not one English Ship hath been built fit for this Trade, the reason whereof is that before mentioned, viz. that it is cheaper freighting of Danes and Easterlins; and it being so, and all men naturally led by their Profit, it seems to me in vain to expect that ever this Law will procure the building of one English Ship fit for that employment, till those Strangers are excluded this Trade for England, and much more improbable it is, that any should now be built than it was formerly, when the Act was first made, because Timber is now at almost double the price in England it was then; The consequence whereof is, That if timely Provision be not made by some additional Law, when our old Stock of Flemish Prizes is worn out, as many of them are already, we shall have very few or no Ships in this Trade.

The Objections which I have heard made to this Proposition, are, viz.

Object. 1. If such an Imposition be laid on those gross Commodities imported by Strangers Ships, that will amount to the excluding all Strangers from this Trade; we shall want Ships in England to carry on the Trade, and so the Commodity will not be had, or else will come very dear to us.

I answer, if the Commodity should be somewhat dearer for the present, it would be no loss to the Nation in general, because all Freight would be paid to English men; whereas the freight paid to Strangers (which upon these Commodities is commonly as much or more then the value of Goods) is all clear loss to the Nation.

2dly, If there should be a present want of Shiping, and the Parliament shall please to enjoyn us to build English Ships for this Trade; This extraordinary good Effect will follow, viz.

It will engage us to do that we never yet did, viz. To fall to building of Fly-boats, (great Ships of burthen of no force, and small charge in sailing) which would be the most profitable undertaking that ever English men were engaged in, and that which is absolutely necessary to be don, if ever we intend to board the Dutch in their Trade and Navigation; these Fly-boats being the Milch-Cows of Holland, from which they have sucked manifoldly greater Profit than from all their Ships of force; though both I know are necessary: But if at first the Parliament shall think fit to enjoyn us only to Ships sailed with an Enlish Master, and three fourths English Marriners, the Danes and Easterlins being by this means put out of so great an Employment for their Shiping, we shall buy Ships proper for this Trade on easie terms of them, perhaps for half their cost, which under value in purchase will be a present clear profit to England.

Object. 2. If this be done in England, may not other Princes account it hard and unreasonable, and consequently Retaliate the like upon us?

To answer this Objection, its necesary to enquire what Kingdom and Country will be concerned in this Law.

1st, Then Italy, Spain and Portugal will be wholly unconcerned.

2dly, So will France, who if they were concerned, can take no offence, while they lay an Imposition of 50 or 60 per Cent upon our Drapery.

3dly, The Dutch and Hamburgers would not by such additional Law be more excluded then now they are, and the latter would have an advantage by it, in case the Danes should (as it may be supposed they will) lay a Tax upon our Shiping there, for the consequence thereof would be, that much of those kind of Commodities we should fetch from Hambrough, where they are plentifully to be had, though at a little dearer Rate, and yet not so dear, but that the Dutch fetch Yearly thence 350, or 400 Ships loading of Timber, and other wooden Commodities.

4thly, The Sweedes would have an apparent benefit by it, by turning a great part of the Stream of our Trade for those Commodities to Gottenborrow, and divers other parts of Sweeden, that are lately opened, and now opening, where very large quantities of Timber, Masts and Boards likewise may be had, though some small matter dearer than in Norway: Besides, if the Sweedes should expect no advantage, but rather loss by such amendment of our own Laws, they have no reason to be angry, because they have lately made so many Laws for encouragement of their own Shiping and Navigation, and consequently discouragement of ours, that do in effect amount to a prohibition of the English from sending their own Manufactures to Sweeden in English Shiping, insomuch that the English Merchants when Sweedish Shiping doth not present, are forced many times to send their Goods to Elsinore, to lie there till a Sweedish Ship come by to put them aboard of, and pay their Factoridge, and other charges, because if they should send them on English Ships, the Duties are so high in Sweeden, that it is impossible for them to make their first cost of them.

5thly, The Easterlins or Hans-Towns, though they were excluded this Trade for England with their Shiping, whereof they have little, (the greatest share being carried away by the Danes) would be gainers by the encrease of our Trade with them, for Boards, Timber, Spruce Deals, &c. at Dantzick, Quinsborough, and other places, which would be very considerable in case the King of Denmark should impose any considerable extraordinary Tribute on our Shiping; which brings me to the third Objection.

Object. 3. If this be done, will not the King of Denmark lay a great Imposition upon all our Shiping that Trade into his Dominions, and also upon our Drapery, and other Native English Commodities.

I answer, That whatever that King may do at first, I am perswaded after he hath considered of it, he will be moderate in his Impositions, because he can hurt none but himself by making them great; for as to Drapery, and other English Goods, his Country spends none worth speaking of, and that charged with about 30 or 40 per Cent Custom already, nine tenths of all the Timber and Boards we fetch from thence, being, in my opinion, purchased with ready Dollars sent from England and Holland; and if he should by a great Imposition totally discourage us from trading with his People, we should lay out that Money with the Sweedes, Hamburgers, Danzickers, and others, where we may have sufficient supply, while the Danes would be exceedingly burthened with the lying of their Goods upon their Hands; there being in Norway great quantities of Goods, viz. the course Hemlock, Timber, commonly brought from Larwick, Tunsberry, Sandyford, Oskestrand, Hollumstrand, and many other parts, which no Nation in the

World trades with them for, or will buy or use but the English only.

A DISCOURSE ABOUT TRADE

TRADE AND INTEREST OF MONEY CONSIDERED, &c.

CHAP. V.

Concerning Transferrance of Debts.

TRADE AND INTEREST OF MONEY CONSIDERED, &c.

CHAP. V.

Concerning Transferrance of Debts.

The great Advantage that would accrue to this Kingdom by a Law for Transferring Bills of Debt, from one person to another, is sufficiently understood by most Men, especially by Merchants.

The difficulty seems not to be so much in making of a Law to this purpose, as reducing it to practice, because we have been so long accustomed to buy and sell Goods by verbal Contracts only, that Rich and Great Men for some time will be apt to think it a Diminution of their Reputation, to have Bills under their Hands and Seals demanded of them for Goods bought; and meaner Men will fear the loosing of their Customers, by insisting upon having such Bills for what they sell, which Inconveniency probably may be avoided, and the Good hoped for fully attained, if it be enacted,

That all and every Person and Persons Native and Foreign, Bodies Politick and Corporate, Being or Inhabiting within the Kingdom of England, or Dominion of Wales, who from and after the day of shall buy and receive any Wares, Goods, and Merchandize from any others, shall immediately on receipt thereof, (in case ready Money be not paid for the same) give unto him or them of whom such Goods, Wares and Merchandize shall be bought, or to his and their use, a Bill or Writing obligatory, under the Hand or Seal of him or them so buying the same, which shall mention the quality of the said Goods, and the neat sum af Money, with the time or times of payment agreed upon.

2. That all Persons, &c. may Transfer the said Bills under their Hands, to any other by a short Assignation on the back side.

3. That every such Assignee may re-assign toties quoties.

4. After such Assignment it shall not be in the power of any Assignor to make void, release or discharge the Debt.

5. No Debts, after Assignment, to be liable to any Attachments, Execution, Statute or Commission of Bankrupt, or other Demand, as the Estate of him or them that Assigned the same.

6. That each Assignment shall absolutely vest the Property into the Assignee, to all intents and purposes.

7. That such Assignments being received, and Receipts or Discharges given for the same, shall be deemed good Payment.

8. That all Goods sold above the value of 10 l. after the day of for which no such Bill or Writing obligatory shall be given or tendred as aforesaid, to the seller or sellers thereof, or to his or their Use, shall be deemed and construed to all Intents and Purposes in the Law, as if the same had been contracted for to be paid in ready Money, any Concession or verbal Agreement between the said Parties to the contrary notwithstanding.

This Clause I hope may be effectual to initiate us to a practice and observance of such a Law.

6. That the first Assignment of any such Bill or Bills of Debt, be to this or the like ffect.

I A. B. do engage and attest, that the Debt within mentioned is a true Debt, and no part of it paid to me or to my use, or discharged by me; and I do hereby Assign over the same to C. D. for his own Account.

10. And that the second, and all other after Assignations upon any such Bills, shall be to this or the like effect, viz.

I A. B. do attest, that no part of the within-mentioned Debt is paid to me or my use, or discharged by me, and I do hereby Transfer the same to C. D.

The Objections I have met with to the making such a Law are, viz.

Object. 1. This would be repugnant to our common Law, and some Statutes, viz. Maintenance, Champarty, Bankrupt, &c.

1. I answer, not so repugnant as at first view it seems to be, for though by our Laws at present, Bonds and Bills cannot be Assigned, Mortgages (which are but another kind of Security for Money lent) may be Assigned.

2. If any Laws at present are repugnant to the common good of the Nation, and if the making of such a new Law will effectually encrease the useful Stock of the Nation, at least one third part, and greatly ease the course of Trade, as I humbly conceive this will do, I hope none will deny but it may consist with the Wisdom of Parliament to create new Laws.

3. Most of our Statutes were made in times before we understood Trade in England, and the same Policy and Laws that were good then, and may yet be good for a Country destitute of Commerce, may not be so fit for us now, nor for any Nation so abounding with Trade as England doth at present.

Object. 2. May not this occasion many Cheats and Law Suites?

Answ. 1. I answer no, Experience manifests the contrary, not only in other Kingdoms and Countries abroad where Transferrance of Bills of Debt is in use, but even in our own where we have for many Ages had the Experience of Indorsment on Bills of Exchange, and in this present Age of the passing of Gold-Smiths Notes from one Man to another, which two practices are very like to the designed way of Transferring Bills of Debt, and yet no considerable Cheats or Inconveniencies have arisen thereby.

Answ. 2. No Man can be Cheated except it be with his own consent, and we commonly say caveat emptor, no Man is to be forced to accept anothers Bill that himself doth not approve of, and no Man will accept of another Mans Bill except he know him, or until he hath used means to satisfie himself concerning him, no more then he will sell his Goods to a Stranger, unless he hath some reason to believe he is able to pay him.

Object. 3. Will not such a Law as this be very troublesom, especially in Fairs and Markets, and also to Gentlemen and Ladies when they shall be forced for all Goods they buy above the value of 10 l. to give Bills under their Hand and Seals?

I answer, this Law will not at all Incomode Gentlemen as to what they Buy in Shops, &c. neither those that converse in Fairs and Markets; for that which Gentlemen Buy in Shops, &c. and others in Fairs, &c. they either pay or promise ready Money, or else say nothing of the time or payment, which the Law understands to be the same with a promise of present pay; so that if they give no Bills, there is no penalty attends the neglect or refusal, but only that the contract between the Buyer and Seller shall be presumed in the Law to be as if it were made for ready Money.

A DISCOURSE ABOUT TRADE

TRADE AND INTEREST OF MONEY CONSIDERED, &c.

CHAP. VI.

Concerning a Court Merchant.

TRADE AND INTEREST OF MONEY CONSIDERED, &c.

CHAP. VI.

Concerning a Court Merchant.

I have conceived great hope from the late most Prudent and Charitable Institution of that Judicature, for determination of Differences touching Houses Burned by the late Fire in London, that this Kingdom will at length be blessed with a happy method, for the speedy, easie and cheap deciding of Differences between Merchants, Masters of Ships and Seamen, &c. by some Court or Courts of Merchants, like those which are established in most of the great Cities and Towns in France, Holland and other places; the want whereof in England, is and hath ever been a great bar to the Progress and Grandure of the Trade of this Kingdom; as for instance, if Merchants happen to have differences with Masters and Owners of Ships, upon Charter-parties or Accounts beyond Sea, &c. The Suite is commonly first commenced in the Admiralty Court, where, after tedious Attendance and vast Expences, probably just before the Cause should come to Determination, it is either removed into the Deligates, where it may hang in suspence until the Plantiff and Defendant have empty purses and grey Heads, or else, because most Contracts for Martain Affairs, are made upon the Land (and most Accidents happen in some Rivers or Harbours here, or beyond Sea, are not in alto mari). The Defendant brings his Writ of Prohibition, and removes the Cause into his Majesties Court of King's-Bench, where after great Expences of Time and Money, it is well if we can make our own Council (being common Lawyers) understand one half of our Case, we being amongst them as in a Foreign Country, our Language strange to them, and theirs as strange to us; after all, no Attestations of Foreign Notaries, nor other publick Instruments from beyond Sea, being Evidences at Law, and the Accounts depending, consisting perhaps of an hundred or more several Articles, which are as so many Issues at Law, the Cause must come into the Chancery, where after many Years tedious Travels to Westminster, with black Boxes and green Bags, when the Plantiff and Defendant have tired their Bodies, distracted their Minds, and consumed their Estates, the Cause if ever it be ended, is commonly by order of that Court referred to Merchants, ending miserably, where it might have had at first a happy issue if it had begun right.

From whence follows these National Inconveniencies.

1. It is a vast Expence to the Persons concerned.

2. It takes off Men from following their Callings, to the Publick loss, as well as the particular Damages of the concerned, that time being lost to the Nation that is spent in Law-Suits.

3. It makes Men, after they have once attained indifferent Estates, to leave Trading, and for ease to turn Country-Gentlemen, whereas great and experienced Men are the only Persons that must mate the Dutch in Trade, if ever we do it.

4. It is my opinion a great cause of the Prodigality, Idleness, and Injustice of many of our Masters of Ships in England, and consequently a wonderful bar to the growth of our English

Navigation, who knowing that their Owners cannot legally eject them, especially if the Master have a part of the Ship himself, but that Remedy to the Owners will be worse then the Disease, which occasions Masters to presume to do those things, and be guilty of such neglects as naturally they would not, if they stood more upon their good behaviour.

I could say much more of the Damage this Nation sustains by the want of a Law-Merchant, but that is so evident to all Mens Experience, that I shall not longer insist upon it, but proceed humbly to propose some particulars, which being duely considered, may peradventure by wiser Heads be improved towards the cure of this evil, viz.

1. That it be Enacted, that there shall be erected within the City of London, a standing Court-Merchant, to consist of twelve able Merchants, such as shall be chosen by the Livery Men of the said City in their common Hall, at the time and in the manner herein after limitted and appointed.

2. That the said twelve persons so to be Elected, or any three or more of them, sitting at the same time and place, and not otherwise, shall be accounted Judiciary Merchants, and Authorized to hear and determine all Differences and Demands whatsoever, which have arisen (and are not hitherto determined) or may any ways arise between Merchants, Trades-Men, Artificers, Masters and Owners of Ships, Sea-Men, Boat-Men and Freighters of Ships, or any other Persons having relation to Merchandizing, Trade or Shiping, for or concerning any Account or Accounts of Merchants, Freight of Ship, or Goods, Bill or Bills of Exchange, or Bills of Bottomry, or Bumery, or for Work done upon, or Materials delivered to the use of any Ship, or Money due for sale of Goods, or any other thing relating to Trade or Shiping.

3. That any three or more of them (as the Judges lately did at Clifford's-Inn) may proceed sumarily to the hearing and

determining of any such Differences, and that their Sentence shall be final, from which there shall be no Appeal or Review, otherwise then as is hereafter mentioned, nor any Writ of Error lie for the removal, or reversal of the same.

4. That they, or any three of them may so issue out Summons for convening all Persons before them, as the Judges did, &c.

5. That they be a Court of Records, as the Judges were, &c.

6. That they take nothing for their own pains, directly or indirectly, but six pence each for Signing every final Order in every Cause, whereof the value of the Money to be paid doth not exceed 10 l. And 12 d. for all Causes not exceeding 100 l. and only 2's. each for all Causes exceeding the value of 100l.

The said Fees to be due and payable only to such and so many of the said Judiciary Merchants as heard the said Cause and Causes, and Signed the Judgments or final Decrees in them.

7. That for Rewards to Officers, the Judiciary Merchants do constitute a Table of reasonable Fees, to be confirmed by the two Lord Cheif-Justices, and Lord Chief Baron of the Exchequer.

8. That in any Case determined by a less number then seven of the said Judiciary Merchants, there may be an Appeal to seven or more, as was lately practised in the afore-mentioned Judicature.

9. That they may have power to levy Executions upon Estates real or personal, with such Restrictions as the Parliament shall please to appoint.

10. That the extent of the Jurisdiction of the said Court, shall be to all Places within ten Miles of London, or only to the late Lines of Communication, as the Parliament shall think fit.

11. That the said Judiciary Merchants and their Officers, before they exercise their Authority, take such Oathes as the Parliament shall please to appoint.

12. That if any of the Judiciary Merchants be Prosecuted for exercising any of the Powers that shall be committed to them, Page 119 they may plead the general Issue, and give the Act in evidence for their Defence.

13. That no Writ or Writs of Supersedeas, Certiorary, or Injunctions out of any of his Majesties Courts, shall superceed, or stay Execution, &c.

14. The Act to continue Probationarily so long as the Parliament shall think fit.

15. That the twelve Judiciary Merchants shall be chosen Yearly by all the Freemen, that are Livery-men of London, in the Guild-Hall of the said City, or by so many of them as shall be present at such Elections, upon every Munday Yearly, next before the Feast day of St Michael (or as the Parliament shall appoint) in manner following, Every Livery-man then present, to deliver unto any two such Aldermen and four Commoners, as the Lord Mayor and Court of Aldermen for the time being, shall appoint to take the view or scruteny of Election, a Paper containing the names of such twelve Persons as he thinks best to be Elected for the purposes afore said, setting his, the said Electors, own name on the back-side of the said Paper, and the next Munday after, in the said Guild-Hall, the said two Aldermen, and four Commoners, or so many of them as shall have taken the Scrutiney, shall publickly declare unto the Lord Mayor, Aldermen and Commoners then present, who are the twelve Persons chosen by the majority of Votes, and how many Votes each of them had.

16. If it happen that any of the judiciary Merchants dye before the end of the Year, or refuse to undertake the Trust, it be lawful for the Livery-men to choose another or others, toties quoties. And the Lord Mayor being enjoyned to summon Common-Halls to that purpose.

17. That every Year six of the old judiciary Merchants go off

in course, and be uncapable of being re-elected, and six new ones chose in their stead, viz. all the twelve to be re-chosen, but only six of the old ones that had the most Voices to hold next Year, although more of them should happen to be elected for the next Year.

Object. 1. The many Objections that I can fore-see will be made against this Constitution, is, that It thwarts that most excellent order of our English Juries.

Answ. 1. I answer, That I hope there is no English man more in love with Juries then my self; but it is evident that the common way of Tryals, doth not well reach the variety and strangeness of Merchants cases, especially in relation to foreign Affairs.

Answ. 2. What better Jury can a Merchant hope for, than twelve able and honest Merchants, chose by the collective Body of the whole City, and such as shall all of them stand upon their Good Behaviour to be turned out with Ignominy the next Year, if they do not equal right to all men.

Object. 2. The admitting of no Appeals from a Court-Merchant seems too arbitrary.

I answer; While we choose our Judges our selves for Merchants cases, and may remove them our selves, in my opinion they can be no more too arbitrary than too much power can be given to Referees, when both parties desire an end of their Differences; besides, if their Power be not great, the many designs of cheap, speedy, and short issues will be lost. But if it shall please the Parliament, there may be in the Act an appeal reserved to the House of Lords the Money condemned, to be first paid or deposited before the Appeal be allowed.

A DISCOURSE ABOUT TRADE

TRADE AND INTEREST OF MONEY CONSIDERED, &c.

CHAP. VII.

Concerning Naturalization.

TRADE AND INTEREST OF MONEY CONSIDERED, &c.

CHAP. VII.

Concerning Naturalization.

That an Act of Naturalization of Strangers would tend to the advancement of Trade, and encrease of the value of the Lands of this Kingdom, is now so generally owned and assented to, by all degrees of men amongst us, that I doubt not but a short time will produce some Act or Acts of Parliament to that purpose. I have therefore thought it not impertinent to note some few Particulars, which if not warily prevented, may deprive us of the greatest part of the Fruit hoped for by so good a design, viz.

1st, The Priviledges of encorporated Cities and Towns.

2dly, More especially the Societies of Artificers and Tradesmen belonging to some Cities and Towns Corporate, such as Weavers, Coopers, and many others, who by vertue of their Charters, pretend to Priviledge and Jurisdiction, not only to the utmost extent of the Liberties of their respective Cities and Towns, but to the distance of ten Miles about them.

3. That branch of the Statute of 5th of Elizabeth, which enacts, That none shall use any manual Occupation that hath

not served an Apprenticeship thereunto, upon which Statute it hath been usual to indict Strangers, work-men that have exercised their Callings in the out-parts of London.

Upon this point of Naturalization, many men make a great doubt, whether it be for publick good to permit the Jews to be Naturalized in common with other Strangers.

Those that are against their admission, who for the most part are Merchants, urge these Reasons;

1. They say the Jews are a subtil People, prying into all kind of Trades, and thereby depriving the English Merchant of that Profit he would otherwise gain.

2. They are a penurious People, living miserably, and therefore can, and do afford to trade for less profit then the English, to the prejudice of the English Merchant.

3. They bring no Estates with them, but set up with their Pens and Ink only; and if after some few Years they thrive and grow rich, they carry away their Riches with them to some other Country (being a People that cannot mix with us) which Riches being carried away) is a publick loss to this Kingdom.

Those that are for the admission of the Jews, say in answer to the aforesaid Reasons, viz.

1st, The subtiller the Jews are, and the more Trades they pry into while they live here, the more they are like to encrease Trade, and the more they do that, the better it is for the Kingdom in general, though the worse for the English Merchant, who comparitively to the rest of the People of England is not one of a thousand.

2dly, The thriftier they live, the better Example to our people; there being nothing in the World more conducing to enrich a Kingdom then thriftiness.

3dly, It is denyed that they bring over nothing with them; for many have brought hither very good Estates, and hundreds more would do the like, and settle here for their Lives, and their Posterities after them, if they had the same Freedom and Security here as they have in Holland and Italy, where the grand Duke of Tuscaney, and other Princes allow them not only perfect Liberty and Security, but give them the priviledge of making Laws among themselves; and that they would reside with us, is proved from the known Principles of Nature, viz.

Principle 1. All men by Nature are alike, as I have before demonstrated, and Mr Hobbs hath truly asserted, how Erroneous soever he may be in other things.

Princip. 2. Fear is the cause of Hatred and hatred of separation from, as well as evil Deeds to the Parties or Government hated, when opportunity is offered: This by the way shews the difference between a bare connivence at Dissenters in matters of Religion, and a toleration by Law; the former keeps them continually in Fear, and consequently apt to Sedition and Rebellion, when any probable occasion of success presents: The latter disarms cunning, ambitious minded men, who wanting a popular discontented Party to work upon, can effect little or nothing to the prejudice of the Government. And this methinks discovers clearly the Cause why the Lutherans in Germany, Protestants in France, Greeks in Turkey, and Sectaries in Holland are such quiet peaceable-minded-men, while our Non-Conformists in England are said to be enclinable to Strife, War and Bloodshed; Take away the Cause, and the Effect will cease.

While the Laws are in Force against men, they think the Sword hangs over their Heads, and are always in fear (though the Execution be suspended) not knowing how soon Councils, or Counsellors, Times or Persons may change, it is only Perfect Love that casts out Fear; and all men are in love with Liberty and Security: It cannot be denyed that the industrious Bees have Stings, (though Drones have not) yet Bees sting not, except those that hurt them, or disturb their Hives.

It is said, the Jews cannot Intermarry with us, and therefore it cannot be supposed they will reside long amongst us, although they were treated never so kindly; why not reside here as well as in Italy, Poland or Holland; they have now no Country of their own to go to, and therefore that is their Country, and must needs be so esteemed by them, where they are best used, and have the greatest Security.

A DISCOURSE ABOUT TRADE

TRADE AND INTEREST OF MONEY CONSIDERED, &c.

CHAP. VIII.

Concerning Wool and Woollen Manufactures.

TRADE AND INTEREST OF MONEY CONSIDERED, &c.

CHAP. VIII.

Concerning Wool and Woollen Manufactures.

That Wool is eminently the Foundation of the English Riches, I have not heard denyed by any, and that therefore all possible means ought to be used to keep it within our own Kingdom, is generally confessed, and to this purpose most of our modern Parliaments have strenuously endeavoured the contriving of severe Laws to prevent its Exportation, and the last Act made it Felony to Ship out Wool, Woolfels, &c.

Notwithstanding which, we see that English and Irish Wool goes over so plentifully, that it is within a very small matter as cheap in Holland as in England.

The means to prevent this Evil, by additional Penal Laws, and alterations of some of those now in being, were long under debate, by his Majesties command in the Council of Trade, who according to their duty, took great pains therein; and since, I have been informed the same things were under consideration in Parliament, so that I doubt not, but in due time we shall see some more effectual Laws enacted to this purpose, as well in relation to Ireland, (from whence the greatest of this mischief proceeds) as in England, then ever yet have been; yet I do utterly despair of ever seeing this Disease perfectly cured till the Causes thereof be removed, which I take to be;

1st, Heighth of Interest in England, which an Abatement by Law to 4 per Cent would cure.

2dly, Want of Hands, which an Act of Naturalization would cure.

3dly, Compulsion in matters of Religion, which some relaxation of the Ecclesiastical Laws, I hope would effectually cure.

For while our Neighbours, through the cheap valuation of their Stocks, can afford to trade, and disburse their Monies for less profit then we, as hath been I think sufficiently demonstrated by the fore-going Discourse, and have more Hands to employ then we, by reason of the large Immunities and Priviledges they give both to Natives and Foreigners, there is no question but they will be able to give a better Price for our Wool, than we can afford our selves; and they that can give the best price for a Commodity shall never fail to have it, by one means or other, notwithstanding the opposition of any Laws, or interposition of any Power by Sea or Land; of such force, subtilty and violence is the general course of Trade.

Object. But some may say, and take it as well from what I have writ elsewhere, as from their own Observations, Will not the well-making of our Woollen-Manufactures, contribute much to the keeping of our Wool naturally within our own Kingdom.

I answer; Doubtless it will have a great tendency thereunto, but can never effect it, till the aforesaid Radical Causes of this Disease be removed, which brings me to the next Question, viz.

What will improve our Woollen-Manufactures in quality and quantity?

This is a very great Question, and requires very deliberate and serious Consideration, but I shall write my present Thoughts concerning it, desiring those Gentlemen's pardon, from whom I may differ in Opinion, having this to say for my self, that I do it not rashly, this being a business that I have many Years considered of, and that not solitarily, but upon converse with the most skilful men in our several English Woollen Manufactures.

1. Then I say, Those three fore-mentioned Particulars which will naturally keep our Wool at home, will as naturally encrease our Woollen-Manufactures.

2. Negatively, I think that very few of our Laws now in force to this purpose (though our Statute-Books are replenished with many) have any tendency thereunto, nor any thing I have yet seen in Print; For,

1st, All our Laws relating to the Aulnegeors duty, every body knows signifie nothing to the encrease, or well-making our Manufactures, but are rather chargeable and prejudicial.

2dly, All our Laws that oblige our People to the making of strong, substantial (and as we call it, Loyal) Cloth of a certain length, breadth and weight, if they were duly put in Execution, would in my opinion do more hurt than good, because the Humors and Fashions of the World change, and at sometimes in some places (as now in most) slight cheap light Cloth will sell more plentifully and better, than that which is heavier, stronger and truer wrought; and If we intend to have the Trade of the World, we must imitate the Dutch, who make the worst as well as the best of all Manufactures, that we may be in a capacity of serving all Markets, and all Humors.

3dly, I conclude all our Laws limitting the number of Loomes numbered, or kind of Servants, and Times of working, to be certainly prejudicial to the cloathing of the Kingdom in general, though they be advantagious to some particular Men or Places, who first procured those Laws of Restriction and Limitation.

4thly, I think all those Laws are Prejudicial, that prohibit a Weaver from being a Fuller, Tucker or Dyar, or a Fuller or Tucker from keeping a Loome.

5thly, I conculde that stretching of Cloth by Tentors, though it be sometimes prejudicial to the Cloth, is yet absolutely necessary to the Trade of England, and that the excess of straining cannot be certainly limitted by any Law, but must be left to the Sellers or Exporters discretion, who best knows what will please his Customers beyond the Seas; besides, if we should wholly prohibit straining of Cloth, the Dutch (as they have often done) would buy our unstrained Cloth, and carry it into Holland, and there strain it to six or seven Yards per piece more in length, and make it look a little better to the Eye, and after that carry it abroad to Turkey, and other Markets, and there beat us out of Trade with our own Weapons.

But some may then ask me, Whether I think it would be for the advantage of the Trade of England, to leave all men at liberty to make what Cloth and Stuffs they please, how they will, where and when they will, of any lengths or sizes?

I answer; Yes, certainly in my judgment it would be so, except such Species only as his Majesty & the Parliament shall think fit to make Staples, as suppose Colchester Bayes, Perpetuanoes, Cheanyes, and some other sorts of Norwich Stuffs to be allowed the honour of a publick Seal, by which to be bought and sold here, and beyond Seas, as if it were upon the publick Faith of England; and where-ever such Seal is allowed, or shall be thought fit to be affixed to any Commodity, I would desire the Commodity should be exactly made according to the Institution, and always kept to its certain length, breadth and goodness.

But in case any shall make of the said Commodities worse

then the Institution, I think it would be most for the publick advantage to impose no Penalty upon them, but only deny them the benefit and reputation of the publick Seal, to such Bayes or Stuffs as shall be so insufficient; which in my opinion would be punishment enough to those that should make worse than the Standard, and advantage enough to those that should keep to it.

2. For all Cloth and Stuffs not being made Staples, I think it would be of very great use that the Makers did weave in their Marks, and affix their own Seals, containing the length and breadth of the Pieces (as hath been provided in some Statutes) and that no Maker under severe Penalties shall use another Mark or Seal, with such Penalty to every marker or seller, whose Cloth or Stuffs shall not contain the length and breadth set upon the Seal, as his Majesty and the Parliament shall think sit.

3. If the makers of all Stuffs whatsoever for Exportation, whether Staples or not (which are commonly sold by the Piece, and not by the Yard or Ell) were obliged to make them no shorter than antiently they have been made; the particular lengths of each sort whereof might be provided for, and expressed in the Act, this good effect would follow upon it, viz.

At all foreign Markets, where we pay a great Custom by the Piece, according to the Books of Rates, currant in the several Countries, we should pay but the same Custom abroad for a piece of full length, which now we do for one that is shorter: Notwithstanding, I conceive it would be expedient to leave it to the makers discretion, to make their pieces as much longer as they please.

A DISCOURSE ABOUT TRADE

TRADE AND INTEREST OF MONEY CONSIDERED, &c.

CHAP. IX.

Concerning the Ballance of Trade.

TRADE AND INTEREST OF MONEY CONSIDERED, &c.

CHAP. IX.

Concerning the Ballance of Trade.

That the Greatness of this Kingdom depends upon Foreign Trade, is acknowledged, and therefore the Interest of Trade not unbecoming Persons of the highest Rank; and of this Study, as well as others, it may be said, there's an infinite in it, none, though of the largest Intelects and Experience, being able to fathom its utmost depth.

Among other things relating to Trade, their hath been much discourse of the Ballance of Trade; the right understanding whereof may be of singular use and serve as a Compass to Stear by, in the Contemplations and Propagation of Trade for publick Advantage.

The Ballance of Trade is commonly understood two ways.

1. Generally, something whereby it may be known whether this Kingdom gaineth or loseth by Foreign Trade.

2. Particularly, something whereby we may know by what Trades this Kingdom gaines, and by what Trades it loseth.

For the first of these.

It is the most general received opinion, and that not ill grounded, that this Ballance is to be taken by a strict Scrutiny of what proportion the value of the Commodities exported out of this Kingdom bear, to those Imported; and if the Exports exceeds the Imports, it is concluded the Nation gets by the general course of its Trade, it being supposed that the over-plush is Imported in Bulloin, and so adds to the Treasure of the Kingdom; Gold and Silver being taken for the measure and standard of Riches.

2. This Rule is not only commonly applyed to the general course of Foreign Trade, but to particular Trades to and from this Nation to any other.

Now although this notion have much of truth in it, was ingeniously and worthily started by him that first published it; and much good hath accrued to the Kingdom by our Law-makers (Noble men and Gentlemen) resenting it, yet if the difficulty of the Scrutiny whereby to reduce it into practice, and the many Accidents that may accrue, be seriously weighed, it will appear too doubtful and uncertain as to our general Trade, and in reference to particular Trades fallible and erroneous.

That it will not hold as to Foreign Trade in general appears;

1. From the difficulty and impossibility of taking a true account, as well of the quantity, as of the value of Commodities Exported and Imported.

The general rule for this hath been the Custom-House-Books, but that they cannot be in any measure certain will easily be granted, for,

1. As to the quantity, if it be considered that many fine Commodities of small bulk and great value, as Points, Laces, Ribands, fine Lennen, Silks, Jewels, &c. are Imported by stealth; & that also in many out-Ports and Creeks of England & Wales, Commodities of bulk are both Imported and Exported often-times by indirect means, that never are Registred, besides

also of what is entered, there may be (though not considerable in London) yet in other parts much difference in the quantities and qualities.

2. As to the value, how shall the compute be made, seeing the rates of the Customs are in no kind proportinable, our own Commodities being some rated very low, as Drapery, Silk-Wares, Haberdashery, and all Manufactures of Iron: Others high, as Lead and Tin; and Fish in English Shiping nothing; and for Foreign Commodities Imported, the rates are yet more unequal, so that the value rated for the Customs cannot be a due measure.

Besides, Foreign Commodities Imported by English Shiping, should be valued only at their first Cost and Charges aboard, and those by Foreign Shiping, with the encrease of the home-ward Freight.

2. From the many Accidents that fall out in Trade, without the true knowledge whereof a right Ballance cannot be made, as,

1. Accidents that diminish the Stock sent out, as losses at Sea, bad Markets, Bankrupt, also Confiscations, Seisures and Arrests, which fall out often on several occasions.

Now if by any of these or such like the original Stock comes to be impaired, and lessened, the value of the Commodities Imported in return, may be far less then the value of the Commodities Exported, and yet may be the full product, and so the Nation no Gainer, though the Exports were more in value then the Imports.

2. Accidents whereby the Stock sent out, comes to be extraordinarily advanced in Sale abroad, from whence it may fall out, that the Commodities Imported in return, may appear to be of a much greater value then the Commodities Exported, and yet be no more then the real produce of them, and so the Nation no loser, but a Gainer thereby, although the Imports

exceeds the Exports.

And if the afore-cited Instances suffice not to prove the uncertainty (in some cases) of this Notion of the Ballance of Trade, the following Examples of Ireland, Virginia and Barbadoes, are so pregnant to this case, as I think will convince any Man: For those three Countries do without doubt Export Annually a far greater value of the Commodities of their native growth and product, then is Imported to them from hence, or from any Foreign Country, and yet they are not such great Gainers, but continue Poor; the true reason whereof as to Ireland, is given by the most Ingenious Author of that Treatise of Taxes and Contributions, Page 27. where he saith, That a great part of Estates both real and personal in Ireland, are owned by Absentees, and such as draw over the Profits raised out of Ireland, refunding nothing; so as Ireland Exporting more then it Imports, doth yet grow Poorer to a Paradox.

Here let me glaunce at my old Theme, and desire the Reader to consider seriously, whether it may not improperly be said of all Kingdoms and Countries, where the Interest of Money runs higher then their Neighbours, that a part of their Estates are owned by Absentees, and consequently they shall be sure to be kept Poor, whether their Importations or their Exportations exceed.

This likewise resolves a Question that was once put to me by an Honourable person concerning the County of Cornwell, which notwithstanding the great quantity of Tin and Pilchards, which Annually the Inhabitants are sending forth from their two Mines of Land and Sea, yet that Country still remains in a poor condition; The reason whereof to me seems clearly to be, because a great part of the Stock imployed in the aforesaid great Trade, is taken up at Interest, and consequently owned by Londoners, and other Absentees.

And though it may be hoped that this is not yet the case of

England, yet it is a demonstration that the notion of takeing the Ballance this way, is not absolutely, and in all places, and under all circumstances, without exception true & good; for in case the Trade of England should be carried on by Absentees, then the supposition upon which this Notion is grounded, (viz. that when the Exports over Ballance the Imports, the Surplusage is returned into England in Bulloin) will prove a mistake, and the contrary will be true, viz. that the Surplusage will be conveighed into Foreign parts, to the places of the residence of such Absentees.

2. The second thing I am to Illustrate is, that this rule (barely considered) is fallible and erroneous, as to particular and distinct Trades.

This will appear, if it be considered, that a true measure of any particular Trade, as to the profit or loss of the Nation thereby, cannot be taken by the consideration of such Trade in it self singlely, but as it stands in reference, and is subservient to the general Trade of the Kingdom; for it may so fall out that there may be some places to which little of our English Manufactures are Exported, and yet the Commodities we have from thence, may be so necessary to the carrying on our Trade in general, or some other particular Trades, that without them the Nation would greatly decline and decay in Trade.

Now in this case, if we should measure such a particular Trade by the aforesaid Notion of the Ballance, we should find the Imports abundantly exceed the Exports, and so be ready to conclude against such a Trade as destructive, whereas (notwithstanding) it may in truth, be a very necessary beneficial Trade, and to the very great advantage of the Nation; as for instance,

The Trade of Denmark and Norway, the Imports from whence are certainly many times the value of our Native Commodities exported thither, and yet it cannot be denied but that Trade is advantagious to the Kingdom, not only because it gives, or would give employment to two Hundred, or three Hundred Sail of English Shiping (if we did a little mend our Act of Navigation) but principally because the Commodities imported from thence, as Timber, Pitch, Deals and Tar, are of such necessary use, in order to the building and supplying our Shiping, that without them other Trades could not be carried on.

It will not be denied by the honourable East-India Company, but they import much more Goods into England, than they export, & that to purchase the same, they carry out quantities of Gold & Silver annually; yet no man that understands any thing of the Trade of the World, will affirm, that England loseth by that Trade. The Dutch with good reason esteem the trade of the East-Indies more profitable to them than are the Mines of Gold and Silver in America to the King of Spain; and if the English Companies were vested by Act of Parliament with so much Authority as the Dutch have, and thereby encouraged to drive as full a Trade thither, as the Dutch do, I doubt not but it would be so (not so much to the private gain of the Members of that Company) as the publick profit of this Kingdom in general; however as it is, it will not be difficult to prove that it is the most beneficial Trade this Nation drives at present; For,

1st, That trade constantly employes twenty five to thirty Sail of the most War-like Ships in England, with Sixty to a Hundred Men in each Ship, and may in two or three Years more employ a greater Number; and in order to the carrying on that Trade, that Company hath lately (unconstrained) given considerable Encouragements for the building of great Ships, which hath had good effect.

2dly, It supplies the Nation constantly and fully, with that (in this Age) necessary material of Salt-Petre.

3dly, It employs the Nation for its Consumption, with

Pepper, Indico, Calicoes, and several useful Drugs, near the value of 150000 l. to 180000 l. per Annum.

4thly, It furnished us with Pepper, Cowryes, Long-Cloth, and other Callicoes and painted Stuffs, proper for the Trade of Turkey, Italy, Spain, France and Guiny, to the amount of 2 or 300000 l. per Annum; most of which Trades we could not carry on with any considerable advantage; but for those supplies, and these Goods exported do produce in foreign parts, to be returned to England, six times the Treasure in Specie, that the Company exports from hence.

Now, if not only the aforesaid advantages be seriously considered, but also what detriment the Nation would sustain, if we were deprived of those supplies, both in point of Strength and War-like Provisions, in regard of Shiping and Salt-Petre, but also in respect of the furtherance it gives to many other Trades before-mentioned, it will easily appear that this Trade, though its Imports exceeds its Exports, is the most advantagious Trade to England, and deserves all encouragement; for were we to buy all our Pepper and Callicoes, &c. of the Dutch, they would raise our Pepper (which now stands the Nation but about 3 d. per pound in India) to, or near the proportion which they have advanced on Nutmegs, Cloves and Mace, (which cost the Dutch not much more per pound in India than Pepper) since they engrossed the Trade for those Commodities; and the use of Callico in England would be supplied by foreign Linnen at greater Prices; so that what may be secured from this Nation's consumption, would in probability cost them above 400000 l. per Annum more then now it doth; and our foreign Trades for Italy, Guiny, &c. would in part decay for want of the afore-said supplies.

There is another Notion concerning the Ballance of Trade, which I think not impertinent here to take notice of, viz. Some are of opinion, that the way to know whether the Nation gets or loseth in the general by its fore-going Trade, is to take an inspection into the course of the Exchange, is generally above the intrinsick value or Par of the Coins of foreign Countries, we not only lose by such Exchanges, but the same is a demonstration that we lose by the general course of our foreign Trade; and that we require more supply of Commodities from abroad, than our exports in Goods do serve to purchase: And certain it is, that when once the Exchange comes to be 5 or 6 per Cent above the true value of foreign Monies, our Treasure would be carried out, whatever Laws should be made to prevent it; and on the contrary, when the Exchange is generally below the true value of the foreign Coins, it is an evidence that our Exports do in value exceed what we require from abroad: And so if the Exchange comes to be 5 or 6 per Cent below the true value of the foreign Coins, returns will be made for England in the Coins of foreign Countries.

Now, that there is also a great deal of truth in this Notion, is not to be denied, and that the diligent observance and consideration of the course of the Exchange, may be of use, and very necessary in many respects, and is a very ingeniuous Study for any that would dive into the mysteries of Trade; yet because this is likewise subject to vary on many accidents of Emergencies of State and War, &c. & because there is no settled course of Exchange, but to and from France, Holland, Flanders, Hambrough, Venice, Legorn & Genoa, and that there are many other great and eminent Trades besides what are driven to those Countries, this cannot afford a true and satisfactory solution to the present Question.

Thus having demonstrated that these Notions, touching the Ballance of Trade, though they are in their kind useful Notions, are in some cases fallible and uncertain. If any shall ask, How shall we then come to be resolved of the matter in Question?

I answer; first, The best and most certain discovery, to my

apprehension, is to be made from the encrease or diminution of our trade and Shiping in general; for if our Trade and Shiping diminish, whatever profit particular men may make, the Nation undoubtedly loseth; and on the contrary, if our Trade and Shiping encrease, how small or low soever the profits are to private men, it is an infallible Indication that the Nation in general thrives; for I dare affirm, and that Catagorically in all parts of the whole World, whereever Trade is great, and continues so, and grows daily more great, and encreaseth in Shiping, and that for a succession not of a few Years, but of Ages, that Trade must be Nationally profitable.

As a Town where only a Fair is kept, if every Year the number of People and Commodities do augment, that Town, however the Markets are, will gain; whereas, if there comes still fewer and fewer People and Commodities, that place will decline and decay. Discoursing once with a Noble Lord concerning this measure or method of knowing the Ballance of our Trade, or more plainly our general National gain or loss by Trade, his Lordship was pleased to oppose, by asking two very proper Questions, viz.

Quest. 1. Is there not a great similitude between the Affairs of a private Person, and of a Nation, the former being but a little Family, and the latter a great Family?

I answer; Yes, certainly there is.

Quest. 2. His Lordships second question was, May not a private Merchant be, or seem to be owner of much Shiping, drive a great Trade, receive and send out many Goods, and yet decline and grow poorer, notwithstanding all his tumbling and busseling?

I answer; Yes, certainly he may, but this will soon appear, either while he lives, or at his Death; and his great Trade will come to be but a small one, or none at all: But that man who drives a great Trade, and is owner or employer of much Shiping, and doth all his dayes continue and encrease in Trade and Shiping, and his Son, or Successor after him, and after him his Grand Son, &c. this would be an indisputable Evidence that that Person or Family did thrive by their Trade; for if they had not thriven, their Trade would not have long continued, muchless encreased: This is the case of Nations, and this through God's goodness is the case of England (as bad as we are at present.)

The reason of this is as evident as the first, for where a great Trade is driven, especially where much Shiping is employed, whatever becomes of the poor Merchant, that drives the Trade, Multitudes of People will be certain gainers, as his Majesty and his Officers of Custom, besides Shipwrights, Butchers, Brewers, Bakers, Rope-makers, Porters, Sea-men, Manufacturers, Carmen, Lighter-men, and all other Artificers, and People that depend on Trade and Shiping, which indeed more or less the whole Kingdom doth.

But it may be said again, If this encrease of Trade depend upon, and proceed from our ordinary Importations, for which our ready Money goes out, it will impoverish us.

I answer, In some cases it may be so, and in some cases (as I have already demonstrated) it may be otherwise, but that will best be known by the effects; for if we are impoverished, our general Trade and our Shiping will necessarily and visibly grow less and less, and must rationally and unavoidably do so; for that being impoverished, we shall lose our Tools (our Stock) to drive a great Trade with; whereas on the contrary, if our Trade in the gross bulk of it (though we may decline in some) do still encrease, especially our Shiping for a long tract of Years, it is infallible proof of our thriving by our Trade, and that we are still getting more Tools (more Stock) to trade with.

Some there are would limit this discovery to the encrease and dimunition of our Coin and Bulloin, but because that is more secret and indiscernable, it cannot, I conceive, afford so clear a demonstration as the other, if any at all, for that Money seems to vulgar Observers most plentiful when there is least occasion for it; and on the contrary, more scarce, as the occasions for the employment thereof are more numerous and advantagious, according to which we should seem to have most Money when we have the least Trade, and yet then certainly the Nation gets least; this is apparent to those that will observe that when the East-India-Company have a great sale to make, then Money is generally found to be scarce in London, not that is so in reality more then at other times, but because that extraordinary occasion engageth men to employ quantities, which they provide and lay aside for that purpose; from the same reason it is, that a high rate of Usury makes Money seems scarce, because every man then, as soon as he can make up a small sum sends it into the Goldsmiths, whereof more is said before in the Preface to this discourse.

I answer, that though the Study of the Ballance of Trade in this last mentioned respect be a Study very Ingenious and Commendable, yet in my poor opinion, the enquiry, whether we get or lose, doth not so much deserve our greatest pains and care, as how we may be sure to get, the former being of no use but in order to the latter, and this therefore leads to the Consideration of the other Ballance of Trade, as most usefull and necessary, viz.

What is to be done in England to improve the Trade thereof to such a degree as to equalize or over-ballance our Neighbours in our National Profit by our Foreign Trade?

I answer, this is a large and extensive Question, and requires to resolve it, the greatest Skill and Experience both in affairs of State and Trade, and therefore I have only made an Essay towards it, which the whole Discourse fore-going is, (and therefore I hope the Reader will accept of my good Affection to my Country herein, though he meet not with that full satisfaction he might expect and wish for.)

The method I propose for the further answering of this great Question, is, (following my own principle) that if Trade be great, and much English Shiping employed, it will be good for the Nation in general, whatever it may be for private Merchants) First to lay down some general Rules for the enlargement of Trade in England, and then some ways of reducing those general Rules into Use and Practice; the general Rules for the enlargement of Trade are not many.

1. Encrease Hands in Trade.

2. Encrease Stock in Trade.

3. Make Trade easie and ncessary, i. e. make it our Interest to Trade.

4. Make it the Interest of other Nations to Trade with us.

1. To encrease Hands in Trades, the following Particulars would much contribute.

1st. An Act of Naturalization before-mentioned.

2. Some enlargement of the Foundations of Societies of Merchants, as before-limitted.

3. A more easie and free admission of Inhabitants, Merchants, and Artificers, to be Burgers of our Cities and Bouroughs.

4. Not to hinder any Man from keeping as many Servants as he can, nor Loomes, working-Tooles, &c.

5. To abate the Interest of Money, as afore-said.

6. Some Relaxation of the Ecclesiastical Laws, would keep our own People at Home, and invite others to us, and consequently encrease the number of our Hands in Trade.

7. Employ, Educate and Relieve the Poor, so as they may neither be Idle, nor perish for Want, or leave the Land by Reason of their Miseries.

8. Giving such Honour and Perferment to Merchants in the Affairs of the Nation, as their Experience & Education hath

fitted them for, will doubtless encrease their number.

Te encrease our Stock in Trade.

1. All the six fore-going particulars, will very much contribute, especially the Abatement of Interest, because bringing in of more Stock, for that the persons engaged in Trade, must necessarily bring in their Stocks with them, if they have any; and for Artificers that have none, their Labour in consequence will generate Stock to the Nation, and encrease that we have already.

2. A Law for Transferrance of Bills of Debt, (as before-mentioned) will much and speedily augment our useful Stock.

3. The restraining of the Trades of our own Plantations wholly to England, and preventing all kind of abuses of that part of the Acts of Trade and Navigation, would tend much to the encrease of our Stock in Trade.

4. The securing of that great Trade for Shiping imployed for Importation of Timber, Masts, Boards and Pipes-Staves into these three Kingdoms, to be done only by his Majestie's Subjects, and not by any Strangers, would in a very few Years much encrease the Stock of England.

5. Prevention of the Exportation of our Wool, and encourageing our Woollen Manufactures.

6. Encourage and encrease our Fishing Trades, which how that is only to be done, is before-mentioned.

7. To set up the Linnen rather then the Woollen Manufacture in Ireland, and give extraordinary encouragement and priviledges to the first Undertakers.

8. To encourage those Trades most, that vent most of our Manufactures, or supply m with Materials to be further Manufactured in England, or else such as furnish us with Commodities for the carrying on of other Trades, as the East-India-Company doth eminently.

9. If his Majesties Navy, Debts, &c. were all paid, and if

for the future, all his Majesties Payments were made with punctuality, it would much encrease the Stock of this Nation in Trade; such fatal stops being to the Body politick, like great obstructions of the Liver and Spleen to the Body Natural, which not only procure ill Habits, but sometimes desperate and accute Diseases, as well as Cronical.

10. Lessening the number of our Holly-Days would encrease the days of our Working, and Working more would make us Richer: Riches and Stock are the same.

11. If our Affairs would permit, that the full Custom should be paid back, &c. (& not the half only) for all Foreign Goods brought hither, and afterwards Exported, (as I am credibly informed the French King hath very lately done in all the parts of his Dominions) it would wonderfully encrease our Navigation, and in consequence our People, as well as our Domestick and Foreign Trade; and in my opinion be much better for the Nation in general, then particular Free Ports.

And if only such Foreign Goods as should be Loaden outwards on English Shiping, had the benefit of this Indulgence, it would be much the more Effications as to our main concern, viz. the encrease and improvement of our English Navigation.

3d. General Rule, To make Trade easie and necessary, and thereby to make it our Interest to Trade.

1. To make Trade easie, a Law for Transferrance of Bills of Debt, will do much (as before)

2. To make Trade easie, a Court-Merchant will do much (as before in that Chapter.

3. Taking of the Burthen of Trade, whereof one is the great trouble and delays in receiving back our Impost at the Custom-House, and the great Charge of Fees to Searchers, Waitors, &c.

4. Reducing Interest of Money to 4 per cent, will make Trade easie to the Borrowers, and to make it necessary, it is the Onum Magnum (as before is said) for while we that are

Merchants, can so easily turn Gentlemen by buying Lands for less then twenty Years purchase, let no Man expect that if we thrive, we will drudge all our days in Trade; or if we would, to be sure our Sons will not.

5. To make Trade easie, and Wool rise, which is always aimed at by our Parliaments; Nothing will conduce so much in times of War, as to appoint sufficient regular Convoys to Merchant Ships, which sometimes have been forced to lie full loaden with Draperies five or six Months in the River for want of Convoys, with the Interest of 6 per Cent. eating upon them; while likewise their Cloth by long lying in the Ships is much damnified, and Merchants cannot buy more of the Clothiers until their Goods are at their selling Ports, which when there arrived Merchants can value themselves upon them by Exchange, and begin a fresh Investment in England.

6. To make Trade easie, some abatement of that rigorous way of pressing Sea-men, which sometimes sweeps away the Officers as well as common men, would much conduce, it being an insuperable discouragement to Merchants to have their ships sometimes manned, and unmanned two or three times in a Voyage before they can get them clear into the Sea, which is not so in Holland.

4th General Rule, To make it the Interest of other Nations to Trade with us.

1. Being in a good condition of Strength at Home, in reference to the Navy, and all other kind of Military preparations for Defence, (and Offence upon just occasion given) will render us Wise and Honourable in the esteem of other Nations, and consequently oblige them not only to admit us the Freedom of Trade with them, but the better terms for, and countenance in the course of our Trade.

2. To make it the Interest of others to Trade with us, we must be sure to furnish them at as cheap or cheaper Rates then

any other Nation can or doth; and this I affirm can never be done without subduing Usury especially, and doing those other things before-mentioned, that will conduce to the encrease of our Hands and Stock, for our being in a condition to sell our Neighbours cheaper then others, must be when it is principally an effect of many Hands and much Stock.

Objection; But it may be said, How shall we profit by this Rule of selling cheap to Foreigners, whereas the contrary is said to be the way to Riches, viz. to sell dear, and buy cheap?

Answ. I answer, in a strict sence it may be so, for the private Merchant; but in this discourse I am designing how our publick National Trade may be so managed, that other Nations who are in Competition with us for the same, may not wrest it from us, but that ours may continue and encrease, to the diminution of theirs; if there were no others to wage with us, we might as the Proverb saith, make our own Markets; but as the case now stands, that all the World are striving to engross all the Trade they can, that other Proverb is very true and applicable, All Covet, All Lose.

3. The well contrivement and management of Foreign Treaties, may very much contribute to the making it the Interest of other Nations to Trade with us, at least to the convincing of Foreign Princes wherein, and how it is their Interest to Trade with us.

4. Publick Justice and Honesty will make it the Interest of other Nations to Trade with us, that is, that when any Commodities pass under a publick common Seal (which is in a kind the publick Faith of the Nation) they may be exact in length, breadth and nature, according to what they ought to be by their Seals.

The like care ought to be taken for the true packing of our Herrings and Pilchards, (formerly mentioned.)

5. If we would engage other Nations to Trade with us, we

must receive from them the Fruits and Commodities of their Countries, as well as send them ours, but its our Interest by Example and other means (not distastful) above all kinds of Commodities to prevent as much as may be, the Importation of Foreign Manufactures.

6. The Venetians being a People that take from us very little of our Manufactures, have prohibited our English Cloth, and from whose Territories we receive great quantities of Currance, purchased with our ready Money; It seems to me advantagious for England, that that Importation, as well as the Importation of wrought-Glasse, drinking-Glasses and other Manufactures from thence, should be discouraged; it being supposed we can now make them as well our selves in England.

The Trade for Cannary-Wines, I take to be a most pernitious Trade to England, because those Islands consume very little of our Manufactures, Fish, or other English Commodities; neither do they furnish us with any Commodities to be further Manufactured here, or re-Exported, the Wines we bring from thence being for the most part purchased with ready Money; so that to my apprehension, something is necessary to be done to compel those Islanders to spend more of our English Commodities, and to sell their Wines cheaper, (which every Year they advance in Price) or else to lessen the Consumption of them in England.

I have in this last Discourse of the Ballance of Trade, as well as in my former, confined my self to write only general Heads and Principles that relate unto Trade in general, not this or that particular Trade; because the several Trades, to several Countries, may require distinct and particular considerations, respecting the time, place, competitors with us and other circumstances to find out, wherein our advantages or disadvantages lie, and how to improve the former, and prevent the latter; but as this would be too great a Work for one Man, so I fear it would make this too great a Book to be well read and considered.

But in the Preface to this Treatise, I have briefly mentioned many particular Trades that we have lost, and are loosing, and by what means, and many Trades that we yet retain and are encreasing, and how it happens to be so, which may give some Light to a clearer Discovery and Inspection into particular Trades, unto which Ingenious Men that have Hearts to serve their Country in this (so necessary Work at this time) may add, and further improve, by the advantage of Abilities to express their Sentiments in a more Intelligible and Pausible Stile; but when I and others have said all we can, A low Interest is, as the Soul to the Body of Trade, it is the Sine qua non to the Prosperity and Advancement to the Lands and Trade of England.

A DISCOURSE ABOUT TRADE

TRADE AND INTEREST OF MONEY CONSIDERED, &c.

CHAP. X.

Concerning Plantations.

TRADE AND INTEREST OF MONEY CONSIDERED, &c.

CHAP. X.

Concerning Plantations.

The Trade of our English Plantations in America, being now of as great Bulk and Employing, as much Shiping as most of the Trades of this Kingdom, it seems not unnecessary to Discourse more at large concerning the Nature of Plantations, and the good or evil consequences of them in relation to this and other Kingdoms; and the rather because some Gentlemen of no mean Capacities, are of Opinion that his Majestie's Plantations abroad, have very much prejudiced this Kingdom by draining us of our People; for the confirmation of which Opinion they urge the Example of Spain, which they say is almost ruined by the Depopulation which the West-Indies hath occasioned; to the end therefore a more particular Scrutiny may be made into this matter, I shall humbly offer my Opinion in the following Propositions, and then give those Reasons of Probability which presently occur to my Memory in confirmation of each Proposition.

1. First I agree, That Lands (though excellent) without

Hands proportionable will not enrich any Kingdom.

2. That whatever tends to the Depopulating of a Kingdom, tends to the Impoverishment of it.

3. That most Nations in the civilized Parts of the World, are more or less Rich or Poor proportionably to the Paucity or Plenty of their People, and not to the Sterility or Fruitfulness of their Lands.

4. I do not agree that our People in England, are in any considerable measure abated by reason of our Foreign Plantations; but propose to prove the contrary.

5. I am of Opinion, that we had immediately before the late Plague, many more People in England then we had before the Inhabiting of Virginia, New-England, Barbadoes, and the rest of our American Plantations.

6. That all Colonies or Plantations do endamage their Mother-Kingdoms, whereof the Trades of such Plantations are not confined by severe Laws, and good executions of those Laws, to the Mother-Kingdom.

7. That the Dutch will reap the greatest advantage by all Colonies issuing from any Kingdom of Europe, whereof the Trades are not so strictly confined to the proper Mother-Kingdoms.

8. That the Dutch (though they thrive so exceedingly in Trade) will in probability never endamage this Kingdom by the growth of their Plantations.

9. That neither the French, Spaniard nor Portugeez are much to be feared on that account, not for the same, but for other causes.

10. That it is more for the advantage of England, that New-found-Land should remain Unplanted, then that Colonies should be sent or permitted to go thither to Inhabit, with a Governour, Laws, &c.

11. That New-England is the most prejudicial Plantation to

the Kingdom of England.

I. That Lands though in their Nature excellently good, without Hands proportionable, will not enrich any Kingdom.

This first Proposition I suppose will readily be assented to by all judicious persons, and therefore for the proof of it, I shall only alledge matter of Fact.

The Land of Palestine, once the Richest Country in the Universe, since it came under the Turks Dominion, and consequently unpeopled, is now become the Poorest.

Andaluzia and Granada, formerly wonderful Rich and full of good Towns, since dis-peopled by the Spaniard by Expultion of the Moors, many of their Towns and brave Country Houses are fallen into Rubbish, and their whole Country into miserable Poverty, though their Lands naturally are prodigiously Fertil.

A Hundred other Instances of Fact might be given to the like purpose.

II. Whatever tends to the populating of a Kingdom, tends to the emprovement of it.

The former Proposition being granted, I suppose this will not be denyed, and of the means (viz. good Laws) whereby any Kingdom, may be populated, and consequently enriched, is in effect the substance and design of all my foregoing Discourse, to which, for avoiding repitition I must pray the Reader's retrospection.

III. That most Nations in the civilized parts of the World, are more or less Rich or Poor, proportionable to the paucity or plenty of their People.

This third is a consequent of the two former Propositions; and the whole World is a witness to the Truth of it: The seven united Provinces are certainly the most populous tract of Land in Christendom, and for their bigness, undoubtedly the richest. England for its bigness, except our Forrests, Wastes and Commons, which by our own Laws and Customs are bared from Improvement, I hope is yet a more populous Country than France, and consequently richer; I say, in proportion to its bigness: Italy in like proportion more populous than France, and richer; and France more populous and rich than Spain, &c.

IV. I do not agree that our People in England are in any considerable measure abated, by reason of our foreign Plantations, but propose to prove the contrary.

This I know is a controverted Point, & do believe that where there is one man of my mind, there may be a thousand of the contrary; but I hope when the following Grounds of my Opinion have been throughly examined, there will not be so many Dissenters.

That very many People now go, and have gone from this Kingdom, almost every Year for these sixty Years past, and have and do settle in our foreign Plantations is most certain. But the first Question will be, Whether if England, had no foreign Plantations for those People to be transported unto, they could or would have stayed and lived at home with us?

I am of Opinion they neither would nor could.

To resolve this Question, we must consider what kind of People they were, and are, that have and do transport themselves to our foreign Plantations.

New-England (as every one knows) was originally inhabitated, and hath since successively been replenisht by a sort of People called Puritans, which could not conform to the Ecclesiastical Laws of England, but being wearied with Church Censures and Persecutions, were forced to quit their Fathers Land, to find out new Habitations, as many of them did in Germany and Holland, as well as at New-England; and had there not been a New-England found for some of them, Germany and Holland probably had received the rest: But Old England to be sure had lost them all.

Virginia and Barbadoes were first peopled by a sort of loose vagrant People, vicious and destitute of means to live at home, (being either unfit for labour, or such as could find none to employ themselves about, or had so mis-behaved themselves by Whoreing, Thieving, or other Debauchery, that none would set them on work) which Merchants and Masters of Ships by their Agents (or Spirits, as they were called) gathered up about the Streets of London, and other places, cloathed and transported, to be employed upon Plantations; and these I say were such, as had there been no English foreign Plantation in the World, could probably never have lived at home to do Service for their Country, but must have come to be hanged or starved, or dyed untimely of some of those miserable Diseases, that proceed from want and Vice; or else have sold themselves for Soldiers, to be knockt on the Head or starved in the Quarrels of our Neighbours, as many thousands of brave English men were in the low Countries, as also in the Wars of Germany, France, and Sweeden, &c. or else if they could, by begging, or otherwise, arrive to the Stock of 2 s. 6 d. to waft them over to Holland, become Servants to the Dutch, who refuse none.

But the principal growth and encrease of the afore-said Plantations of Virginia and Barbadoes happened in, or immediately after our late Civil Wars, when the worsted party, by the fate of War, being deprived of their Estates, and having some of them never been bred to labour, and other made unfit for it by the lazy habit of a Soldiers life, there wanting Means to maintain them all abroad with his Majesty, many of them betook themselves to the afore-said Plantations, and great numbers of Scotch Soldiers of his Majesty's Army, after Worcester Fight, were by the then prevailing Powers voluntarily sent in thither.

Another great swarm, or accession of new Inhabitants to the afore-said Plantations, as also to New-England, Jamaica, and all other his Majesties Plantations in the West-Indies, ensued upon his Majesties Restauration, when the former prevailing party being by a divine Hand of Providence brought under, the Army disbanded, many Officers dis-placed, and all the new purcharsers of publick Titles, dispossest of their pretended Lands, Estates, &c. many became impoverished, destitute of employment; and therefore such as could find no way of living at home, and some which feared the re-establishment of the Ecclesiastical Laws, under which they could not live, were forced to transport themselves, or sell themselves for a few Years, to be transported by others to the foreign English Plantations: The constant supply that the said Plantations have since had, hath by such vagrant loose People, as I before-mentioned, picked up, especially about the Streets and Suburbs of London, and Westminster, and by Malefactors condemned for Crimes, for which by the Law they deserved to dye; and some of those People called Quakers, banished for Meeting on pretence of Religious Worship.

Now, if from the Premises, it be duly considered what kind of Persons those have been, by which our Plantations have at all times been replenished, I suppose it will appear that such they have been, and under such Circumstances, that if his Majesty had had no foreign Plantations, to which they might have resorted, England however must have lost them.

To illustrate the truth whereof a little further, let us consider what Captain Graunt the ingenious Author of the Observations upon the Bills of Mortality, saith, pag. 76. and in other places of his Book, concerning the City of London; and it is not only said, but undeniably proved, viz. That the City of London, let the Mortality be what it will, by Plague, or otherwise, repairs its Inhabitants once in two Years. And pag. 101. again, If there be encouragement for a hundred Persons in London (that is, a way how a hundred may live better then in the Country) the evacuating of a fourth or third part of that number must soon be supplied out of the Country, who in a short time remove themselves from thence hither, so long until the City for want of receipt and encouragement, regurgitates and sends them back.

1. What he hath proved concerning London, I say of England in general, and the same may be said of any Kingdom or Country in the World.

Such as our employment is for People, so many will our People be; and if we should imagin we have in England employment but for one hundred People, and we have born and bred amongst us one hundred and fifty People; I say, the fifty must away from us, or starve, or be hanged to prevent it, whether we had any foreign Plantations or not.

2. If by reason of the accommodation of living in our foreign Plantations; we have evacuated more of our People then we should have done, if we had no such Plantations, I say, with the aforesaid Author in the case of London; and if that Evacuation be grown to an excess (which I believe it never did barely on the account of the Plantations) that decrease would procure its own Remedy; for much want of People would procure greater Wages; and greater Wages, if our Laws gave encouragement, would procure us a supply of People without the charge of breeding them, as the Dutch are, and always have been supplied in their greatest Extremities.

Object. But it may be said, Is not the Facility of being transported into the Plantations, together with the enticing Methods customarily used to perswade People to go thither, and the encouragement of living there with a People that speak our own Language, strong Motives to draw our People from us; and do they not draw more from us, then otherwise would leave us, to go into foreign Countries, where they understand not the Language?

I Answer; 1st, It is not much more difficult to get a passage to Holland, than it is to our Plantations.

2dly, Many of those that go to our Plantations, if they could not go thither, would and must go into foreign Countries, though it were ten times more difficult to get thither then it is; or else, which is worse (as hath been said) would adventure to be hanged, to prevent begging or starving, as too many have done.

3. I do acknowledge that the facility of getting to the Plantations, may cause some more to leave us, than would do if they had none but foreign Countries for refuge: But then if it be considered that our Plantations spending mostly our English Manufactures, and those of all sorts almost imaginable, in egregious quantities, and employing near two thirds of all our English Shiping, do therein give a constant Sustenance to it, may be two hundred thousand Persons here at home; then I must needs conclude upon the whole matter, that we have not the fewer, but the more People in England, by reason of our English Plantations in America.

Object. 2. But it may be said, Is not this inferring and arguing against Sence and Experience? Doth not all the World see that the many noble Kingdoms of Spain in Europe, are almost depopulated and ruinated, by reason of their Peoples flocking over to the West-Indies? And do not all other Nations diminish in people after they become possessed of foreign Plantations?

Ans. 1. I answer, With submission to better Judgments, that in my opinion, contending for Uniformity in Religion hath contributed ten times more to the depopulating of Spain, then all the American Plantations: What was it but that which caused the expulsion of so many thousand Moores who had built and inhabited most of the chief Cities and Towns in Andaluzia, Granada, Aragon, and other parts? What was it but that, and the Inquisition that hath and doth daily expel such vast numbers of rich Jews with their Families and Estates into Germany, Italy, Turkey, Holland and England? What was it but that which caused those vast and long Wars between that King and the low Countries, and the effusion of so much Spanish Blood and Treasure, and the final loss of the seven Provinces, which we now see so prodigious, rich and full of People, while Spain is empty and poor, and Flanders thin and weak, in continual fear of being made a prey to their Neighbours.

2. I answer; We must warily distinguish between Country & Country; for though Plantations may have drained Spain of People, it does not follow that they have or will drain England or Holland, because where Liberty and Property are not so well preserved, and where Interest of Money is permitted to go at 12 per Cent, there can be no considerable Manufacturing, and no more of Tillage and Grazing, than as we Proverbially say, will keep Life and Soul together; and where there is little Manufacturing, and as little Husbandry of Lands, the profit of Plantations, viz. the greatest part thereof will not redound to the Mother-Kingdom, but to other Countries wherein, there are more Manufactures and more Productions from the Earth; from hence it follows, Plantations thus managed prove drains of the People from their Mother-Kingdom; whereas Plantations belonging to Mother-Kingdoms or Countries, where Liberty and Property is better preserved, and Interest of Money restrained to a low rate, the consequence is, that every person sent abroad with the Negroes and Utensils, he is constrained to employ, or that are employed with him; it being customary in most of our Islands in America, upon every Plantation, to employ eight or ten Blacks for one White Servant; I say, in this case we may reckon, that for Provisions, Clothes and Houshold-Goods, Sea-men, and all others employed about Materials for building, fitting and victualling of Ships, Every English man in Barbadoes or Jamaica creates employment for four men at

home.

3dly, I answer, That Holland now sends as many, and more people yearly to reside in their Plantations, Fortresses and Ships in the East-Indies (besides many into the West-Indies) than Spain, and yet is so far from declining in the Number of their people at home, that it is evident they do monstruously encrease; and so I hope under the next Head, to prove that England hath constantly encreased in People at home, since our settlement upon Plantations in America, although not in so great a proportion as the Dutch.

V. I am of Opinion that we had immediately, before the late Plague, more People in England, than we had before the inhabiting of New-England, Virginia, Barbadoes, &c?

The proof of this at best I know can but be conjectural; but in confirmation of my Opinion, I have, I think, of my mind the most industrious English Calculator this Age hath produced in publick, viz. Captain Graunt in the fore-mentioned Treatise, pag. 83. his words are,

Upon the whole matter we may therefore conclude, that the people of the whole Nation do encrease, and consequently the decrease of Winchester, Lincoln, and other like places, must be attributed to other Reasons then that of refurnishing London only.

2. It is manifest by the afore-said worthy Author's Calculations, that the Inhabitants of London, and parts ajacent have encreased to almost double within this sixty Years, and that City hath usually been taken for an Index of the whole.

I know it will be said, that although London have so encreased, other parts have as much diminished, whereof some are named before; but if to answer the diminution of Inhabitants in some particular places, it be considered how others are encreased, viz, Yarmouth, Hull, Scarbrough, and other Ports in the North; as also Liverpoole, Westchester and

Bristol; Portsmouth, Lime and Plimouth; and withal, if it be considered what great Improvements have been made these last sixty Years upon breaking up and enclosing of Wastes, Forrests and Parks, and draining of the Fenns, and all those places inhabited and furnished with Husbandry, &c. then I think it will appear probable that we have in England now, at least had before the late Plague, more People then we had before we first entred upon foreign Plantations, notwithstanding likewise the great Numbers of men which have issued from us into Ireland; which Country, as our Laws now are, I reckon not among the number of Plantations profitable to England, nor within the limits of this discourse, although peradventure something may be pickt out of these Papers, which may deserve consideration in relation to that Country.

But it may be said, If we have more People now then in former Ages, how came it to pass that in the times of King Henry the fourth and fifth, and other times formerly, we could raise such great Armies, and employ them in foreign Wars, and yet retain a sufficient number to defend the Kingdom, and cultivate our Lands at home?

I answer; first, The bigness of Armies is not alwayes a certain Indication of the numerousness of a Nation, but sometimes rather of the nature of the Government and Distrubation of the Lands; as for instance, Where the Prince and Lords are owners of the whole Territory, although the People be thin, the Armies upon occasion may be very great, as in East-India, Turkey, and the Kingdoms of Fesse and Morocco, where Taffelet was lately said to have an Army of one hundred and fifty, or two hundred thousand men, although every body knows that Country hath as great a scarcety of people as any in the World: But since Free-holders are so much encreased in England, & the servile Tenures altered, doubtless it is more difficult, as well as more chargeable to draw great numbers of men into foreign Wars.

2. Since the Introduction of the new Artillery of Powder, Shot and Fire-Arms in the World, all War is become as much rather an expence of Money as Men, and success attends those that can most & longest spend Money, rather than men; and consequently Princes Armies in Europe are become more proportionable to their Purses then to the Numbers of their People.

VI. That all Colonies and foreign Plantations do endamage their Mother-Kingdoms, whereof the Trades of such Plantations are not confined to their said Mother Kingdoms, by good Laws and severe Execution of those Laws.

1. The practice of all the Governments of Europe witness to the truth of this Proposition. The Danes keep the Trade of Izland to themselves: The Dutch, Surrenham, and all their Settlements in East-India: The French St Christophers, and their other Plantations in the West-Indies: The Portugeeze, Brazil, and all the Coasts thereof: The Spaniards, all their vast Terriories upon the Main in the West Indies, and many Islands there; and our own Laws seem to design the like, as to all our Plantations in New-England, Virginia, Barbadoes, &c. although we have not yet arrived to a compleat and effectual Execution of those Laws.

2. Plantations being at first furnished, and afterwards successively supplied with People from their Mother Kingdoms, and people being Riches, that loss of people to the Mother Kingdoms be it more or less, is certainly a damage, except the employment of those People abroad, do cause the employment of so many more at home in their Mother Kingdoms, and that can never be, except the Trade be restrained to their Mother Kingdom, which will not be doubted by any that understands the next Proposition, viz.

VII. That the Dutch will reap the greatest advantage by all Colonies, issuing from any Kingdom in Europe, whereof the Trades are not so strictly confined to their proper Mother Kingdoms.

This Proposition will readily be assented unto by any that understand the nature of low Interest and low Customs, where the Market is free, they shall be sure to have the Trade that can sell the best penny-worths, that buy dearest and sell cheapest, (which Nationally speaking) none can do but those that Money at the lowest rate of Interest, and pay the least Customs, which are the Dutch; and this is the true cause why, before the Act of Navigation, there went ten Dutch Ships to Barbadoes for one English.

VIII. That the Dutch (though they thrive so exceedingly in Trade) will in probability never endamage this Kingdom by the growth of their Plantations.

1. In fact the Dutch never did much thrive in planting, for I do remember they had about twenty Years past, Tabago, a most fruitful Island in the West-Indies, apt for the production of Sugars, and all other Commodities that are propagated in Barbadoes, and as I have heard Planters affirm, better accomodated with Rivers for Water-Mills, which are of great use for grinding of the Canes; this Island is still in their possession, and Corasoa, and some others, and about sixteen or seventeen Years past they were so eager upon the Improvement of it, that besides what they did in Holland they set up Bills upon the Exchange in London, proffering great Priveledges to any that would Transport themselves thither. Notwithstanding all which to this day, that Island is not the tenth part so well improved as Jamaica hath been by the English within these five Years; neither have the Dutch at any other time, or in any other parts of the World, made any emprovement by Planting; what they do in the East-Indies being only by War, Trade and Building of Fortified Towns and Castles upon the Sea-Coasts, to secure the sole Commerce of the Places, and with the people,

which they Conquer not, by clearing, breaking up of the Ground, and Planting as the English have done.

This I take to be a strong Argument of Fact to my present purpose.

2. The second Argument to prove this Proposition is from Reason: I have before-mentioned the several Accidents and Methods by which our Foreign Plantations have from time to time come to be peopled and emproved.

Now the Dutch being void of those Accidents, are destitute of the occasions to emprove Foreign Plantations by diging and delving as the English have done.

For 1st. In Holland their Interest and Custom being low, together with their other Encouragements to Trade, mentioned in the former part of this Treatise, gives Employment to all their people born and bred amongst them, and also to multitudes of Foreigners.

2. Their giving Liberty, or at least Connivance to all Religions, as well Jews and Roman-Catholicks, or Sectaries, gives security to all their Inhabitants at home, and expels none, nor puts a necessity upon any to Banish themselves upon that account.

3. Their careful and wonderful providing for and employing their Poor at home, puts all their People utterly out of danger of Starving, or necessity of Stealing, and consequently out of fear of Hanging; I might add to this, that they have not for a long time had any Civil War among them, and from the whole conclude, that the Dutch as they did never, so they never can or will thrive by planting; and that our English Plantations abroad are a good effect, proceeding from many evil causes.

IX. That neither the French, Spaniards or Portugeeze are much to be feared on the account of Planting, not for the same, but for other Reasons.

That the French have had footing in the West-Indies almost

as long as the English is certain, and that they have made no considerable Progress in Planting is as certain; and finding it so in fact, I have been often exercising my thoughts about enquiry into the reason thereof, which I attribute especially to two.

First, because France being an absolute Government, hath not until very lately, given any countenance or encouragement to Navigation and Trade.

Secondly and principally, because the French Settlements in the West-Indies have not been upon Free-Holders as the English are, but in subjection to the French West-India Company, which Company being under the French King, as Lord Proprietor of the places they settle upon, and taxing the Inhabitants at pleasure as the King doth them, it is not probable they should make that succesful Progress in Planting; Propriety, Freedom and Inheritance being the most effectual Spurs to Industry.

2. Though some (who have not looked far into this matter) may think the Spaniards have made great Progress in Planting, I am of opinion, that the English since the time they set upon this Work, have cleared and emproved fifty Plantations for one, and Built as many Houses for one the Spaniards have Built; this will not be very difficult to imagine, if it be considered.

First, that it is not above fifty or sixty Years since the English intended the Propagating Foreign Plantations.

Secondly, that the Spaniards were Possessed of the West-Indies about our King Henry the 7th's time, which is near two Hundred Years past.

Thirdly, that what the Spaniard hath done in the West-Indies, hath been ten times more by Conquest then by Planting.

Fourtly, That the Spaniards found in the West-Indies most of the Cities and Towns ready Built and Inhabited, and much of the Ground emproved and cultivated before their coming thither.

Fifthly, That the Inhabitants which they found there, and subdued, were such a People with whom some of the Spaniards could and have mixed, from whence hath proceeded a Generation of People which they call Mestises; whereas the English, where they have set down and Planted, either found none, or such as were meer wild Heathen, with whom they could not, nor ever have been known to mix.

Sixthly, That now after such a long series of time, the Spaniards are scarce so Populous in any Part of the West-Indies, as to be able to bring an Army of Ten Thousand Men together in a Months time.

From all which I conjecture;

1st. That his Majesty hath now more English Subjects in all his Foreign Plantations, in sixty Years, than the King of Spain hath Spaniards in all his, in two Hundred Years.

2d. That the Spaniards Progress in Planting bears no Proportion to the encrease of the English Plantations.

3d. That seeing the Spaniards, in the time of their greatest Prosperity, and under so many Advantages, have been such indifferent Planters, and have made such slow progress in Peopleing those parts of the West-Indies which they possess, It is not much to be feared that ever the English will be mated by the Spaniards in their Foreign Plantations, or Production of the Native Commodities of those Parts.

Now the reasons why the Spaniards are so thin of people in the West-Indies, I take to be such as these following, viz.

First and principally, because they exercise the same Policy and Governments, Civil and Ecclesiastical in their Plantations, as they do in their Mother-Kingdom; from whence it follows that their People are few and thin abroad, from the same causes as they are empty and void of people at home; whereas although we in England vainely endeavour to arrive at a Uniformity of Religion at home, yet we allow an Amsterdam Liberty in our

Plantations.

It is true, New-England being a more independant Government from this Kingdom then any other of our Plantations, and the People that went thither more one peculiar Sort or Sect, then those that went to the rest of our Plantations, they did for some Years past, exercise some Severities against the Quakers, but of late they have understood their true Interest better, insomuch as I have not heard of any Act of that kind for these five or six Years last, notwithstanding I am well informed, that there are now amongst them many more Quakers and other Dissenters from their Forms of Religious Worship, then were at the time of their greatest Severity, which Severity had no other effect but to encrease the New-English Non-conformists.

2d. A second reason why the Productions of the Spanish West-India Commodities are so inconsiderable in respect to the English, and consequently why their Progress in Planting, hath been, and is like to be much less then the English, as also the encrease of their People, I take to be the dearness of the Freight of their Ships, which is four times more then our English Freight, and if you would know how that comes to be so, twelve per cent Interest will go great way towards the satisfying you, although there are other concomitant lesser causes, which whosoever understands Spain, or shall carefully read this Treatise, may find out themselves.

3d. A third reason I take to be the greatness of the Customs in Old-Spain, for undoubtedly high Customs do as well dwarf Plantations as Trade.

4th. The Spaniards Intense and singular Industry in their Mines for Gold and Silver, the working wherein destroys abundance of their people, at least of their Slaves, doth cause them to neglect in great measure Cultivating of the Earth, and producing Commodities from the growth thereof, which might give employment to a greater Navy, as well as sustenance to a far greater number of people by Sea and Land.

5th. Their multitude of Fryers, Nuns and other reclust and Ecclesiastical Persons which are prohibited from Marriage.

3. The third sort of People I am to Discourse of, are the Portugeeze, and and them I must acknowledge to have been great Planters in the Brazeils and other Places; but yet if we preserve our People and Plantations by good Laws, I have reason to believe, that the Portugeeze (except they alter their Politicks, which is almost impossible for them to do) can never bear up with us, muchless prejudice our Plantations.

That hitherto they have not hurt us, but we them, is most apparent, for in my time we have beat their Muscovado and Paneal Sugars quite out of use in England, and their Whites we have brought down in all these Parts of Europe in price, from seven and eight pounds per l. to fifty Shillings and three Pounds per l. and in quantity; whereas formerly their Brazeil-Fleets consisted of One hundred, to One hundred and twenty thousand Chests of Sugar, they are now reduced to about Thirty thousand Chests, since the great encrease of Barbadoes.

The reason of this decay of the Portugeeze Productions in Brazeils, is certainly the better Policy that our English Plantatitions are founded upon.

That which principally dwarfs the Portugeeze Plantations is the same before-mentioned, which hinders the Spaniards, viz. extraordinary high Customs at home, high Freights, high Interest of Money, Ecclesiastical persons, &c.

From all that hath been said concerning Plantations in general, I draw these two principal Conclusions.

1st. That our English Plantations may thrive beyond any other Plantations in the World, though the Trades of all of them were more severely limitted by Laws and good Execution of those Laws to their Mother-Kingdom of England, exclusive to Ireland and New-England.

2dly. That it is in his Majesties power, and the Parliaments, if they please, by taking off all Charges from Sugar, to make it more intirely an English Commodity, then white-Herrings are a Dutch Commodity, and to draw more profit to this Kingdom thereby, then the Dutch do by that: And that in consequence thereof, all Plantations of other Nations must in a few Years sink to little or nothing.

X. That it is more for the Advantage of England that New found Lands should remain unplanted, then that Colonies should be sent or permitted to go thither to Inhabit under a Governour, Laws, &c.

I have before discoursed of Plantations in general, most of the English being in their nature much a like, except this of New-found-Land, and that of New-England, which I intend next to speak of.

The advantage New-found-Land hath brought to this Kingdom, is only by the Fishery there, and of what vast concernment that is, is well known to most Gentlemen and Merchants, especially those of the West parts of England, from whence especially this Trade is driven.

It is well known, upon undeniable poof, that in the Year, 1605. the English employed 250. Sail of Ships small and great, in Fishing upon that Coast; and it is now too apparent, that we do not so employ from all Parts, above Eighty Sail of Ships.

It is likewise generally known and confessed, that when we employed so many Ships in that Trade, the current price of our Fish in that Country, was (Communibus annis) seventeen Rials, which is eight Shillings six Pence per Qunital, and that since, as we have lessened in that Trade, the French have encreased in it, and that we have annually proceeded to raise our Fish from seventeen Rials to twenty four Rials, or twelve Shillings, (Communibus annis) as it now sells in the Country:

This being the Case of England in relation to this Trade, it is certainly worth the enquiery.

1st. How we came to decay in that Trade.

2dly, What means may be used to recover our antient Greatness in that Trade, or at least to prevent our further diminution therein?

The decay of that Trade I attribute.

First and principally, to the growing Liberty which is every Year more and more used in Romish Countries, as well as others, of eating Flesh in Lent and on Fish-days.

2. To a late abuse crept into that Trade, (which hath much abated the expence within these twenty Years of that Commodity) of sending over private Boat-keepers, which hath much diminished the number of the Fishing-Ships.

3. To the great encrease of the French Fishery of Placentia and other Ports on the back-side of New-found-Land.

4. To the several Wars we have had at Sea within these twenty Years, which have much empoverished the Merchants of our Western Parts, and reduced them to carry on a great part of that Trade at Bottumry, viz. Money taken upon Adventure of the Ship at twenty per cent per Annum.

2. What means may be used to recover our antient greatness in that Trade, or at least to prevent our farther diminution therein.

For this, two contrary ways have been propounded,

1. To send a Governour to reside there, and to encourage people to Inhabit there, as well for Defence of the Country against Invasion, as to manage the Fishery there by Inhabitants upon the Place, this hath often been propounded by the Planters and some Merchants of London.

2. The second way propounded, and which is directly contrary to the former is, by the West-Country Merchants and Owners of the Fishing-Ships, and that is to have no Governour

nor Inhabitants permitted to reside at New-found-Land, nor any Passengers, or private Boat-keepers suffered to Fish at New-found-Land.

This latter way propounded is most agreeable to my Proposition, and if it could be effected, I am perswaded would revive the decaied English-Fishing-Trade at New-found-Land, and be otherwise greatly for the advantage of this Kingdom, and that for these following reasons,

1. Because most of the Provision the Planters which are settled at New-found-Land, do make use of viz. Bread, Beef, Pork, Butter, Cheese, Clothes, and Irish-Bengal Cloth, Linnen and Woollen; Ireish-Stockings, as also Nets, Hooks and Lines, &c. they are supplied with from New-England and Ireland; and with Wine, Oyl and Linnen by the Salt Ships from France and Spain, in consequence whereof the Labour, as well as the Feeding and Clothing of so many Men is lost to England.

2. The Planters settled there, being mostly loose vagrant People, and without Order and Government, do keep dissolute Houses, which have Debaucht Sea-Men, and diverted them from their laborious and industrious Calling; whereas before there were settlements there, the Sea-Men had no other resort during the Fishing Season (being the time of their abode in that Country) but to their Ships, which afforded them convenient Food and Repose, without the Inconveniencies of Excess.

3 If it be the Interest of all Trading Nations principally to encourage Navigation, and to promote especially those Trades which employ most Shiping: then which nothing is more true, nor more regarded by the wise Dutch, then certainly it is the Interest of England to discountenance and abate the number of Planters at New-found-Land, for if they should encrease, it would in a few Years happen to us, in relation to that Country, as it hath to the Fishery at New-England, which many Years since was managed by English Ships from the Western Ports; but as

Plantations there encreased, fell to be the sole Employment of People settled there, and nothing of that Trade left the poor old English-Men, but the liberty of carrying now and then by courtesie or purchase, a Ship loading of Fish to Bilvoa, when their own N w-English Shiping are better Employed, or not at leisure to do it.

4. It is manifest that before ther were Boat-keepers or Planters at New-found-land Fish was sold cheaper than now it is, by about 40 per Cent, and consequently more vented, the reason whereof I take to be this; The Boat-keepers and Planters, being generally at first able Fisher-men, and being upon the place, can doubtless afford their Fish cheaper then the Fishing Ships from Old England, so doubtless they did at first as well at New-England as at New-found-land, until they had beat the English Ships out of the Trade; after which being freed from that competition, they became Lazy as to that laborious employment, having means otherwise to live and employ themselves, and thereupon enhaunced the price of their Fish to such an excess, as in effect proves the giving away of that Trade to the French, who by our aforesaid impolitick management of that Trade, have of late Years been able to under-sell us at all Markets abroad; and most certain it is, that those that can sell cheapest will have the Trade.

5. This Kingdom being an Island, it is our Interest, as well for our preservation as our profit, not only to have many Sea-men, but to have them as much as may be within call in a time of danger. Now the Fishing Ships going out in March, and returning home for England in the Month of September yearly, and there being employed in that Trade two hundred and fifty Ships, which might carry about ten thousand Sea-men, Fisher-men and Shore men, as they usually call the younger Persons, which were never before at Sea: I appeal to the Reader, whether such a yearly return of Sea-men, abiding at home with us all the

Winter, and spending their Money here which they got in their Summer-Fishery, were not a great access of Wealth and Power to this Kingdom, and a ready supply for his Majesty's Navy upon all Emergencies.

6. The Fishing Ships yet are, and always have been the breeders of Sea-men; the Planters and Boat-keepers are generally such as were bred, and became expert at the cost of the Owners of Fishing Ships, which Planters and Boat-keepers enter very few new or green men.

7. By the building, fitting, victualling and repairing of Fishing-Ships, multitudes of English Trades-men and Artificers (besides the Owners and Sea-men) gain their subsistance; whereas by the Boats, which the Planters and Boat-keepers build or use at New-found-Land, England gets nothing.

Object. But against all that I have said, those that contend for a Governour at New-found-Land, object;

1. That without a Governour and Government there, that Country will be alwayes exposed to the surprizal of the French, or any Foreigners that shall please to attacque it.

2. That the disorders of the Planters, which I complain of (and some others, which for brevities sake, I have not mentioned) cannot be remedied without a Governour.

To which I answer, first, That when we cannot preserve our Colonies by our Shiping, or so awe our Neighbours by our Fleets and Ships of War, that they dare not attempt them, our case will be sad, and our Propriety will be lost, or in eminent danger, not only abroad, but at home likewise.

2dly, All the Fish that is killed at New-found-Land in a Summer, is not sufficient to maintain strength enough on Shore to defend two Fishing Harbours against ten men of War, whereas that Country hath more Harbours to defend, than are to be found in Old England.

3dly, If a Governour be established, the next consequence

will be a Tax upon the Fishing, and the least Tax will encrease the price of Fish, and that unavoidably will give the Trade away wholly into the French Hands.

4thly, A Government there is already of antient Custom among the Masters of the Fishing-Ships, to which the Fishermen are inured, and that free from Oppression, and adapted to the Trade, insomuch that although a better might be wished, I never hope to see it.

XI That New-England is the most prejudical Plantation to this Kingdom.

I am now to write of a People, whose Frugality, Industry and Temperance, and the happiness of whose Laws and Institution, do promise to themselves long Life, with a wonderful encrease of People, Riches and Power: And although no men ought to envy that Vertue and Wisdom in others, which themselves either can or will not practice, but rather to commend and admire it; yet I think it is the duty of every good man primarily to respect the well-fare of his Native Country; and therefore though I may offend some, whom I would not willingly displease, I cannot omit in the progress of this discourse, to take notice of some particulars, wherein Old England suffers diminution by the growth of those Colonies settled in New-England, and how that Plantation differs from those more Southerly, with respect to the gain or loss of this Kingdom, viz.

1. All our American Plantations, except that of New-England, produce Commodities of different Natures from those of this Kingdom, as Sugar, Tobacco, Cocoa, Wool, Ginger, sundry sorts of dying Woods, &c. Whereas New-England produces generally the same we have here, viz. Corn and Cattle; some quantity of Fish they do likewise kill, but that is taken & saved altogether by their own Inhabitants, which prejudiceth our New found-land Trade, where, as hath been said, very few are, or ought according to Prudence, to be employed in those

Fisheries, but the Inhabitants of Old England.

The other Commodities we have from them, are some few great Masts, Furs, and Train-Oyl, whereof the Yearly value amounts to very little, the much greater value of returns from thence, being made in Sugar, Cotton, Wool, Tobacco, and such like Commodities, which they first receive from some other of his Majesty's Plantations, in Barter for dry Cod-Fish, salt Mackerel, Beef, Pork, Bread, Beer, Flower, Pease, &c. which they supply Barbadoes, Jamaica, &c. with, to the diminution of the vent of those Commodities from this Kingdom; the great Experience whereof in our own West-India Plantations, would soon be found in the advantage of the value of our Lands in England, were it not for the vast and almost incredible supplies those Colonies have from New-England.

2. The People of New-England, by vertue of their Primitive Charters being not so strictly tied to the observation of the Laws of this Kingdom, do sometimes assume a liberty of Trading, contrary to the Act of Navigation, by reason whereof many of our American Commodities, especially Tobacco and Sugar, are transported in New-English Shiping, directly into Spain, and other foreign Countries, without being Landed in England, or paying any Duty to his Majesty, which is not only loss to the King, and a prejudice to the Navigation of Old England; but also a total exclusion of the old English Merchant from the vent of those Commodities in those Ports, where the New-English Vessels trade; because, there being no Custom paid on those Commodities in New-England, and a great Custom paid upon them in Old England, it must necessarily follow that the New-English Merchant will be able to afford his Commodity much cheaper at the Market, than the Old English Merchant: And those that can sell cheapest, will infallibly engross the whole Trade sooner or later.

3. Of all the American Plntations, his Majesty hath none

so apt for the building of Shiping as New-England, nor none comparably so qualified for the breeding of Sea-men, not only by reason of the natural industry of that people but principally by reason of their Cod and Mackerel Fisheries: And in my poor opinion, there is nothing more prejudicial, and in prospect more dangerous to any Mother Kingdom, then the encrease of Shiping in their Colonies, Plantations or Provinces.

4. The People that evacuate from us to Barbadoes, and the other West-India Plantations, as was before hinted, do commonly work one English man to ten or eight Blacks; and if we kept the trade of our said Plantations intirely to England, England would have no less Inhabitants, but rather an encrease of people by such evacuation, because that one English man, with the ten Blacks that work with him, accounting what they eat, use and wear, would make employment for four men in England, as was said before; whereas, peradventure of ten men that issue from us to New-England & Ireland, what we send to, or receive from them, doth not employ one man in England.

To conclude this Chapter, and to do right to that most Industirous English Colony, I must confess that though we loose by their unlimitted Trade with our Foreign Plantations, yet we are very great Gainers, by their direct Trade to and from Old England. Our Yearly Exportations of English Manufactures, Mault and other Goods from hence thither, amounting in my opinion to ten times the value of what is Imported from thence, which Calculation I do not make at randum, but upon mature Consideration, and peradventure upon as much Experience in this very Trade, as any other person will pretend to; and therefore, when ever a Reformation of our Correspondency in Trade with that people shall be thought on, it will in my poor Judgment require great Tenderness & very serious Circumspection.

FINIS.

A DISCOURSE ABOUT TRADE

A SMALL TREATISE AGAINST USURY.

A DISCOURSE ABOUT TRADE

A SMALL TREATISE AGAINST USURY.

To leave the proofs of the unlawfulness of Usury to Divines, wherein a number, as well Protestants as Papists, have learnedly Written; here is only set down some Arguments to shew how great the hurt is it doth to this Kingdom, which hath no Gold nor Silver Mines, but plenty of Commodities, and many and great Advantages of Trade; to which the high rate of Usury is a great prejudice and decay.

For proof how much the high rate of Usury decays Trade; we see that generally all Merchants when they have gotten any great Wealth, leave Trading, and fall to Usury, the gain thereof being so easie, certain, and great; whereas in other Countries, where Usury is at a lower rate, and thereby Lands dearer to purchase, they continue Merchants from Generation to Generation, to inrich themselves and the State.

Neither are they rich Trades-Men only, that give over Trading, but a number of Beginners are undone or discouraged by the high rate of Usury, their Industry serving but to Enrich others, and Begger themselves.

We also see many Trades themselves much decayed, because they will not afford so great a gain as Ten in the Hundred;

whereas, if the rate of Usury were not higher here then in other Countries, they had still subsisted and flourished, and perhaps with as much Advantage to the Publick, as those that do bring more to the private Adventurers.

Yet are not those the greatest hinderances the high rate of Money brings to Trade; our greatest disadvantage is, that other Nations, especially our Industrious Neighbours the Dutch, are therein Wiser then we: For with them, and so in most Countries with whom we hold Commerce, there is not any Use for Money tollerated, above the rate of Six in the Hundred: Whereby it must of necessity come to pass, though they have no other Advantages of Industry and Frugality, that they must out-Trade us; for if they make return of ten per Cent, they almost double the Use allowed, and so make a very gainful Trade. But with us, where ten in the Hundred is so currant, it is otherwise; for if we make not above ten, we are loosers, and consequently the same Trade being with them and us equally good for the Publick, is to the private Adventurers lossful with us, with them very gainful. And where the good of Publick and private Mens go not together, the Publick is seldom greatly advanced.

And as they out-Trade, so they may afford to under-sell us in the Fruits of the Earth, which are equally natural to our and their Lands, as to our great shame we see our Neighbours the Dutch do, even in our own Country: For in most Commodities the Earth brings forth, the Stock imployed in Planting and managing of them, makes a great (in many the greatest) part of their Price; and consequently, their Stock with them, being rated at six in the Hundred, they may with great Gain under-sell us, our Stock with us being rated at ten.

And as they may out-Trade us and under-sell us, so are all Contributions to the War, works of Piety and Glory of the State, cheaper to them then to us, For the Use for Money going with us near double the rate it doth in other Countries, the giving the same Sum must needs be double the charge to us it is to them.

Amongst other things which the King, with so much Wisdom, delivered to the House of Parliament, he committed to their Consideration the Ballancing of Trade and Commerce, wherein there is nothing of greater consequence, then the rate of Usury, which holds no Proportion with us and other Nations, to our disadvantage, as by Experience we see and feel.

Neither is the high rate of Usury less hurtful to Commerce within the Land, the Gain by Usury being so easie, certain, and extream great, as they are not only Merchants and Trades-men, but Landed-men, Farmers, and men of Profession that grow Lazy in their Professions, and become Usurers; for the rate of Usury is the measure by which all men Trade, Purchase, Build, Plant, or any other ways bargain.

It hath been the Wisdom and Care of former Parliaments to provide for the preservation of Wood and Timber; for which there is nothing more available then the calling down of the high rate of Usury; for as the rate of Money now goeth, no man can let his Timber stand, nor his Wood grow to such years growth as is best for the Common-Wealth, but it will be very lossfull to him; The stock of the Woods after they are worth forty or fifty Shillings the Acre, growing faster at ten in the Hundred, then the Woods themselves do.

And for Shipping, which is the strength and safety of this Land; I have heard divers Merchants of good Credit say, that if they would Build a Ship, and let it to any other to imploy, they cannot make of their Money that way, counting all charges, tear and wear, above ten or twelve in the Hundred, which can be no gainful Trade, Money it self going at ten in the Hundred.

But in the Low-Countries, where Money goeth at six, the Building of Ships, and Hiring them to others, is a gainful Trade; and so the Stock of rich Men, and the Industry of Beginners, are well joyned for the Publick.

And yet that which is above all the rest, the greatest Sin against the Land is, that it makes the Land it self of small value, nearer the rate of new-found Lands, than of any other Country, where Laws, Government, and Peace, have so long flourished; for the high rate of Usury makes Land sell so cheap; and the cheap sale of Land is the cause Men seek no more by Industry and Cost to improve them.

And this is plain both by Example, and Demonstration: For we see in other Countries, where the Use of Money is of a low rate, Lands are generally sold for thirty, forty, in some for fifty Years Purchase.

And we know by the rule of Bargaining, that if the rate of Use were not greater here, then in other Countries; Lands were then as good a penny worth at twenty Years Purchase, as they are now at sixteen: For Lands being the best Assurance and securest Inheritance, will still bear a rate above Money.

Now if Lands were at thirty Years Purchase, or near it, there were no so cheap Purchase as the Amendment of our own Lands; for it would be much cheaper to make one Acre of Land, now worth five Shillings by the Year, to be worth ten Shillings, or being worth ten to be worth twenty Shillings, and so in Proportion; then to purchase an other Acre worth five or ten Shillings.

And in every Acre thus purchased to the Owner, by the amendment of his own, there were another purchased to the Common-Wealth.

And it is the Blessing of God to this Land, that there are few places of it to which he hath not given means, by reasonable Cost and Industry, greatly to amend it, in many to double the value, so as in time, if for their own good, mens Industry were compelled that way, the Riches and Commodities of this Land will near be doubled.

Then would all the wet Lands in this Kingdom soon be drained, the barren Lands mended by Marle, Sleech, Lime, Chalk, Sea-sand, and other means, which for their profit, mens industry would find out.

We see with how great industry and charge our Neighbours, the Dutch, do drain and maintain their Lands against the Sea, which floweth higher above them, then it doth above the lowest parts of our drown'd Lands.

I will admit a great deal to their Industry, but I should very unwillingly grant, that they are so much more ingenuous and industrious then we, as that all the odds were therein.

Certainly, the main cause of it is, that with us Money is dear, and Land cheap; with them Land is dear, and Money cheap; and consequently the Improvement of their Lands at so great a charge with them, is gainful to the Owners, which with us would be lossful; for Usury going at ten in the Hundred, if a man borrow five Pounds, and bestow it on an Acre of Ground, the amendment stands him in ten Shillings the Year, and being amended, the Land is not worth above fifteen Years purchase.

But if the Use of Money went at no more with us, then in other places, then five Pound bestowed upon an Acre of Gound, would stand a man but in five or six Shillings a Year, and the Acre of Land so amended, would be worth, as hath been shewed, six and twenty or thirty years purchase.

Whereby it appeareth that as the rate of Use now goeth, no man (but where the Land lieth extraordinarily happily for it) can amend his Land, but to his own loss; whereas if Money were let as it is in other Countries, he might bestow more then double so much as now he may, and yet be a great gainer thereby; and consequently, as was before remembred, should to his own benefit purchase Land to the Common-wealth.

Neither would such purchase of Land to the Common-wealth, be the benefit to the Landed men only, the benefit would be as much to the poor Labourers of the Land: For now when Corn and other Fruits of the Land, which grow by labour, are cheap, the Plough and Mattock are cast into the Hedge, there is little work for poor men, and that at a low rate; whereas, if the mendment of their own Lands were the cheapest purchase to the Owners; if there were many more people then there are, they should more readily be set a work, at better rates then they now are, and none that had their Health and Limbs could be poor, but by their extreamest laziness.

And as the high rate of Usury doth imbase Lands, so it is as great a hindrance to Discoveries, Plantations, and all good undertakings, making it near double as chargeable to the Adventurers, (Money being at ten in the hundred) as it is in other Countries, where the Use of Money is so much lower.

Now let us see by the contrary, and conceive if Usury were tollerated at fifteen or twenty in the hundred (and I fear many Borrowers, all things considered, pay above ten) what the condition of things would then be, and if it appear how desperate the hurt would be which that would bring; it may (at least upon good reason) perswade us how great the good would be of calling it down.

Certainly, it must of necessity come to pass, that all Trades would in a short time decay; For few or none (and reckon the hazard at nothing) yield so great a gain as twenty in the hundred; and all other Nations might with so great gain out-trade and under-sell us, that more than the Earth would of her self bring forth, we should scarce raise any thing from it, even for our own use within the Land; and Land would be so much imbased, as men might afford without loss to themselves, to carry the Compost out of their Closes, upon their next adjoyning Lands to mend them: so far should we be from Marling, Liming, Draining, Planting, and any other works of Cost or Industry, by which Lands are purchased to the Common-wealth. So far from building, making of Havens, Discoveries, new Plantations, or any other actions of Vertue and Glory to the State; for private gain is the Compass men generally sail by.

And since we cannot, without extraordinary diligence, Plant, Build, Drain, or any other way amend our Lands, but it will be dearer to us, than the purchase of others, Money being at ten in the Hundred; if Money then should go at twenty in the Hundred, the charge of mending our Land would be doubled, and the Land abased to seven or eight Years purchase; and consequently all works of Industry and Charge, for improving of Lands, would be quite neglected and given over: We should only eat upon one another with Usury, have our Commodities from other Nations, let the Land grow barren and unmanured, and the whole State in short time come to beggary.

Against this (perhaps) may be objected, That before the 37 of H. 8. there was no limitation of Usury, and how did we then?

To this may be answered, That in those times there was a stricter Band in that point upon Mens Consciences: So far forth as Usurers were in the same case as Excommunicate Persons, they could make no Wills, nor were allowed Christian Burial.

Therefore let us, for our Fore-fathers sake, hope, that the tie upon their Consciences then was a greater Restraint of Usury, than the Statute of ten in the Hundred is now. I fear Fornication is too frequent among us; yet, thanks be to God, not so much used as where there is allowance of Curtizans and Stews.

The Objections likely to be made against the calling down of Money, are,

First, That general Objection of Ignorance against all Changes, be they never so necessary and apparently good, that it hath been so a long time, and been well enough; what will become of the alteration we cannot tell; why then should we make any change?

Secondly, That as in Bodies Natural, so in Politique, great and sudden Changes are most commonly dangerous.

Thirdly, That Money will be suddenly called in, and so all Borrowers greatly prejudiced.

Fourthly, That Money will be harder to come by, and thereby Commerce greatly hindred.

Lastly, That much Money of Foreigners, by Reason of the high rate of Usury, is brought over here to be managed at Interest, which would be carried away again, if the Rate of Usury should be called down.

To the First.

That Money hath long gone at Ten, and things been well enough.

It is answered, That it is not long that the practice of Usury hath been so generally used, without any sence or scruple of the unlawfulness of it; for mens Consciences were hardened to it with example and custom, by degrees, and not upon the sudden.

And as the beginning of many dangerous Diseases in healthful Bodies, so the beginning of many Inconveniencies in a State, are not presently felt.

With us, after that with long Civil Wars the Land was half unpeopled, so as till of late Years, it came not to his full stock of People again, there being the same quantity of Land to half the number of People, the surplusage of our In-land Commodities must needs be so great, that though Trade were not equally ballanced with us and other Nations, we could not but grow rich.

Besides, France and the Low-Countries were for many Years half laid waste with Wars, and so did trade but little, nor manage their own Lands to their best advantage; whereby they did not only not take the Trade & Market from us which now they do, but they themselves were fed and cloathed by us, and took our Commodities from us at great high great Rates.

Whereas now we see the Dutch do every where out-trade us, and the French feed us with their Corn, even in plentiful Years.

So as now our Land being full stocked with People, our Neighbours industrious and subtle in Trade, if we do not more equally Ballance Trade, and bring to pass that we may afford the Fruits of our Land, as cheap as other Countries afford the same of the same kind; we must (though we leave a number of our superfluities, as God forbid but we should) in a short time grow Poor and Beggarly.

And in this condition ten in the Hundred, in a little more time, will as well serve to do it, as if Money were at twenty: For (as was before remembred) in most of the Commodities the Earth bringeth forth, the Stock employed in Planting and managing of of them, makes a great part of their Price; and consequently, they may, with great Gain to themselves, undersell us; our Stock with us going at double the rate that theirs goes with them.

And this we see and feel too well by Experience at this present; for having a great surplusage of Corn, we can find no vent for it; the French with their own, the Dutch with the Corn of Poland, every where supplying the Markets at cheaper rates than we can afford it.

And even our Cloaths, which have hitherto been the Golden Mine in England, I have heard many Merchants say, That (except it be in some few of the finest sort of them, which is a Riches peculiar to this Nation) other Countries begin to make them of their own Wool, and by affording them cheaper then we may, so to take our Markets from us.

And this I hope may in part serve for Answer to the next Objection; that all great and sudden Changes are commonly dangerous; for that Rule holds true, where the Body Natural or Politick is in perfect state of Health, but where there is a declining, (as I have some cause to fear there is, or may soon be with us) there to make no alteration is a certain way to Ruin.

To the Third.

That Money will be suddenly called in, and so all Borrowers greatly prejudiced.

For that there may be a clause in the end of the Statute whensoever it shall be made: That it shall be lawful for all that have lent Money at ten in the Hundred, which is now forborn, and owing, to take for such Money so lent, and owing, during two Years after this Session of Parliament, such Use as they might have done if this Act had not been made: Whereby Borrowers shall be in less danger of sudden calling in of their Money, then now they are; for where the Lenders upon continuance of their old Security, may take ten in the Hundred; upon new Security they may be content with less, so the calling in of their Money will be to their own prejudice.

And if there be any Borrower to whom this giveth not sufficient Satisfaction, if such Borrower have Lands of value to pay his debt, the worst condition he can fear, is to have at the least twenty Years Purchase for his Land, wherewith to clear his Debts; for as I said before, Land being the best Security, and securest Inheritance, will still bear a rate above Money.

And so there being no Use allowed for Money above the rate tollerated in other Countries, Land will as readily sell at twenty Years Purchase, as it doth now at twelve. And I think there is no

Borrower that hath Land of value to pay his Debts, doth doubt if he will now sell his Land at ten Years Purchase, he might soon be out of Debt.

To the fourth Objection.

That Money will be hard to be borrowed, and so Commerce hindred.

I answer, That it were true, if the high rate of Usury did increase Money within this Land; but the high rate of Usury doth enrich only the Usurer, and impoverish the Kingdom, as hath been shewed; and it is the plenty of Money within the Land that maketh Money easie to be borrowed, as we see by the Examples of other Countries, where Money is easier to be borrowed then it is with us, and yet the rate tollerated for Use, is little more then half so much.

It is the high rate of Use that undoeth so many of the Gentry of the Land, which maketh the number of Borrowers so great; and the number of Borrowers must of necessity make Money the harder to be borrowed, whereas if Use for Money were at a lower rate, Land as hath been shewed, would be much quicker to be sold, and at dearer rates, and so the Nobility and Gentry would soon be out of Debt, and consequently the fewer Borrowers, and so to Trades-men and Merchants Money easie to be had.

Further, let us consider if Money were called down, what Usurers would do with their Money; they would not I suppose long be sullen, and keep it a dead stock by them; for that were not so much as the safest way of keeping it: They must then either imploy it in Trade, purchase Land, or lend for Use at such rate as the Law will tollerate: If it quicken Trade, that is the thing to be desired; for that will enrich the Kingdom, and so make Money plentiful.

And yet need not any Borrower fear that Money will so be imployed in Trade, as that there will not be sufficient of Money to purchase Land; where the Purchaser may have as much, or near so much Rent by the purchase of Land, as he can by putting his Money to Use: For a great number of Gentlemen and other in the Country, know not how to imploy any stock in Trade, but with great uncertainty, and less satisfaction to themselves, then the letting of their Money at a lower rate, or purchasing Land at twenty Years purchase or upwards.

No doubt for the present there would be great buying and selling of Land, till Men had cleared themselves, and payed their Debts: But in short time Land, as it is shewed before, would sell at so dear a rate, as Money let at a lower rate of Use, would bring in proportion as great a rate above the Rent that would be made then by the purchase of Land, as the rate of Money now is above the Rent of Land, purchased at fourteen or fifteen Years purchase, and so by consequence Money would then as easily be borrowed as it is now, and so much easier, as it would be more plentiful, and fewer Borrowers.

To the last and weakest of Objections.

That there is now much Money of Foreigners in the Land, to be managed at ten in the Hundred, which if Money should be called down, would be carried out of the Land.

There is no doubt it is true: But I desire to know, whether any man think it better for the State, that they should now carry out one hundred Pounds, or seven years hence, two; or fourteen years hence four; or one and twenty years hence eight: For so in effect upon the multiplying of Interest they do.

It will seem incredible to such as have not considered it, but to any that will but cast it up, it is plainly manifest, that a hundred Pounds managed at ten in the hundred, in seventy years, multiplies it self to a hundred thousand pounds. So if there should be an hundred thousand pounds of Foreigners Money now managed here at ten in the hundred, (and that doth seem no great matter) that an hundred thousand pound in threescore and ten years, which is but the age of a man, would carry out ten Millions, which I believe is more then all the Coin at this present in the Land.

I know we cannot conceive how any such sum should be managed at Interest, yet this is sufficient to make us little to joy in Foreigners Money.

Besides, we must not conceive that the Money of Foreigners which is here managed at Usury, is brought into the Land in ready Coin or Bullion: The course is, That Merchants send over Bills of Exchange to their Factors, for which they receive our Money here; and this is the Money they manage at Interest, and so they eat us out with our own Money.

The old comparison, which compares Usury to the Butlers Box, deserves to be remembred; Whilst men are at play, they feel not what they give to the Box; but at the end of Christmass it makes all, or near all, Gamesters loosers: And I fear the comparison hold thus much farther, That there is as few escape that continue in Usury, as that continue Gamesters; a man may play once or twice, and leave a Winner, but the use of it is seldom without ruin.

Now because I know mens private Interests doth many times blind their Judgments, and lest any may be tempted for their own, against the publick Good; I will desire them to remember, that if they have Lands as well as Money, that what they lose in their Money, they shall get it in their Land; for Land and Money are ever in Ballance one against the other; and where Money is dear, Land is cheap; and where Money is cheap, Land is dear.

And if there be any yet so hearty a well-wisher to ten in the hundred, as that he still thinks it fit to be continued, my wish is, That he and his Posterity may have the priviledge to borrow, but not to lend at that rate.

In the baginning of this Treatise, I did disclaim the proofs of the unlawfulness of Usury, leaving them to Divines, this one only (rising from the Premises) which may serve for all, I think fit to set down:

It is agreed by all the Divines that ever were, without exception of any; yea, and by the Usurers themselves, That biting Usury is unlawful: Now since it hath been proved that ten in the hundred doth bite the Landed men, doth bite the Poor, doth bite Trade, doth bite the King in his Customs, doth bite the Fruits of the Land, and most of all the Land it self; doth bite all works of Piety, of Vertue, and Glory to the State; no man can deny but ten in the hundred is absolutely unlawful, howsoever happily a lesser rate may be otherwise.

To the King, increase of his Customs.

To the Kingdom, increase of Land, by inriching of this.

To the Nobility and Gentry, deliverance from Bondage and Debt.

To Merchants, continuance and flourishing in their Trades.

To young Beginners in Trade and Commerce, the fruits of their own Labours.

To Labourers, quick imployment.

To Usurers, Land for the Money.

A DISCOURSE ABOUT TRADE

POSTSCRIPT

A DISCOURSE ABOUT TRADE

POSTSCRIPT

Since the fore-going Papers were delivered to the Press, Mr Henry Dakers Merchant, sent me a most rational and admirable Treatise concerning Trade, called ENGLAND's INTEREST AND IMPROVEMENT, writ by Samuel Fortrey, Esq one of the Gentlemen of the Majesties Privy Chamber, in which he mentions something concerning the Interest of Money, in the following Words, pag. 42. Viz.

In the last place, concerning the Use of Money; which being the Life and Sinews of Trade, it hath been the Opinion of some, that the greater Use were allowed for Money, the more would be the profit of the Publick; for that Strangers finding a greater benefit to be made of their Money here, than other where, would send it hither, whereby Money would be much more plentiful amongst us.

Indeed I should be of their Opinion, if as soon as by this means great sums of Money were transported hither, all their Money should be confiscate to the Publick: But if otherwise, sure it cannot be denied, but the greater the Use, the more the Profit to the Usurer, and loss to the Debtor, so as in a few Years we should find our selves so little inriched thereby, that when the Principal should be again recalled, we should find but little Money left; all our own being wasted in Use. Wherefore indeed the true benefit to the Publick, is, To set the Use of Money as low, or rather lower than in our Neighbour Countries it is; for then they would make no Profit out of us by that means, but rather we on them. And it is the clear profit that we get of our own, that will make this Nation rich, and not the great sums we are indebted to others.

Which I have here inserted, for such like Reasons:

First, That the World may see I am not singular in this Opinion, although I thought I had been so, when first I wrote the afore-said Observations.

Secondly, For Confirmation of the Truth, by the Authority of a Person of such known Abilities.

Thirdly, To give the Author his due Honour of being the first Observer, &c.

And I am sorry I know not the ingenious Author of the former Tract, that I might do right to his Memory, Who hath done more for his Country than would have been the Gift of some Millions of Pounds Sterling, into the Publick Exchequer.

FINIS.

ALSO AVAILABLE FROM NEWTON PAGE

ALSO AVAILABLE FROM NEWTON PAGE

Nicholas Barbon, The Complete Works
Economics, Trade, Building and Insurance

Nicholas Barbon

ISBN-13: 978-1934619186

Contains each of the six previously inaccessible works authored by Barbon: A Discourse Shewing the Great Advantages that New-buildings and the Enlarging of Towns and Cities do Bring to a Nation (1678); A Letter to a Gentleman in the Country, Giving an Account of the Two Insurance - Offices; the Fire-Office & Friendly-Society (1684); An Apology for the Builder: or a Discourse Shewing the Cause and Effects of the Increase of Building (1685); A Discourse of Trade (1690); An Answer to Paper Entituled, Reasons against Reducing Interest to Four per Cent (1694); and A Discourse Concerning Coining the New Money lighter. In Answer to Mr. Lock's Considerations about raising the Value of Money (1696).

ALSO AVAILABLE FROM NEWTON PAGE

John Law of Lauriston

Financier and Statesman, Founder of the Bank of France, Originator of the Mississippi Scheme

A. W. Wiston-Glynn

ISBN-13: 978-1934619032

The true story of a Scottish murderer, philanderer, gambler and abscondee who escaped his condemned cell in London to become the darling of the French economy, John Law of Lauriston is an account of the euphoria and wealth Law created by engineering the first stock market boom, and the despair, poverty and destruction which followed its inevitable crash.

ALSO AVAILABLE FROM NEWTON PAGE

The Mississippi Bubble

A Memoir of John Law

Adolphe Thiers

ISBN-13: 978-1934619056

An established classic and authoritative historical analysis of the spectacular rise and fall of the most enigmatic genius in financial and economic history. It provides a compelling biographical narrative of John Law's life, a considered examination of his Mississippi Scheme, and enlightening accounts of both the Darien Expedition and South Sea Bubble.

ALSO AVAILABLE FROM NEWTON PAGE

The Life of John Law

Including a Detailed Account of the Rise, Progress and Termination of the Mississippi System

John Phillip Wood

ISBN-13: 978-1934619018

One of the most cited biographies of John Law in existence. It is both a concise and gripping retelling of the extraordinary life story of the 'first millionaire' and also a very readable and entertaining account of the remarkably swift rise and even swifter decline of both of his influential innovations: the Mississippi Company and the Mississippi Scheme.

ALSO AVAILABLE FROM NEWTON PAGE

Letters to John Law

A Letter to Mr. Law
The Case of Mr. Law Truly Stated
A Second Letter to Mr. Law

Selected and introduced by

Gavin John Adams

ISBN-13: 978-1-934619087

This collection of three uncompromising early eighteenth-century propagandist pamphlets documents the wildly contrasting reactions to Law's surprise return to Britain. Crafted by the most prominent journalists, commentators and political agitators of the day, each provides an invaluable contemporaneous social, political and historical record of the most remarkable story in financial history.

ALSO AVAILABLE FROM NEWTON PAGE

The Financier Law

His Scheme and Times: A Graphic Description of the Origin, Maturity and Wreck of the Mississippi Scheme

André Cochut

ISBN-13: 978-1934619049

A richly contextual narrative of the life of John Law, a charismatic Scottish economist and murderer and who would escape execution and use his seemingly effortless financial genius to rise from obscurity to become the most powerful member of the French court, the controller of the French economy, and the richest man the modern world had ever seen.

ALSO AVAILABLE FROM NEWTON PAGE

John Law

The Lauriston Lecture and Collected Writings

Gavin John Adams

ISBN-13: 978-1-934619155

A collection of six unique accounts of the extraordinary life of John Law of Lauriston and the operation of his infamous Mississippi Scheme. In addition to the first lecture on the life of John Law to be delivered at Law's ancestral home of Lauriston Castle, also included in this collection are accounts of his life and the Mississippi Scheme by some of the most popular writers of the last 250 years, including: Bram Stoker, the gothic novelist; Washington Irving, the essayist and short story writer; Charles Mackay, the journalist; Adam Smith, the economist; and Voltaire, the enlightenment writer, historian and philosopher.

Made in United States
Orlando, FL
04 November 2026

90204185R00150